We Can Do IT

This book is number ten in the Litwin Books Series on Gender and Sexuality in Information Studies, Emily Drabinski, Series Editor.

We Can Do IT

Women in Library Information Technology

Edited by

Jenny Brandon
Sharon Ladenson
Kelly Sattler

Library Juice Press
Sacramento, CA

Library Juice Press
PO Box 188784
Sacramento, CA 95818

http://libraryjuicepress.com

This book is printed on acid-free paper.

Library of Congress Cataloging-in-Publication Data

Names: Brandon, Jenny, editor. | Ladenson, Sharon, editor. | Sattler,
    Kelly, editor.
Title: We can do I.T. : women in library information technology / edited by
    Jenny Brandon, Sharon Ladenson, and Kelly Sattler.
Description: Sacramento, CA : Library Juice Press, 2018. | Series: Gender
    and sexuality in information studies ; number 9 | Includes
    bibliographical references and index. | Summary: "A collection of
    personal narratives exploring issues faced by women in information
    technology jobs in libraries, reflecting on themes including imposter
    syndrome, career trajectory, and experiences of sexism. Includes advice
    and encouragement to women entering the field"-- Provided by publisher.
Identifiers: LCCN 2018008670 | ISBN 9781634000536 (paperback : alk. paper)
Subjects: LCSH: Women library employees--United States. |
    Libraries--Information technology--Social aspects--United States.
Classification: LCC Z682.4.W65 W4 2018 | DDC 020.82--dc23
LC record available at https://lccn.loc.gov/2018008670

Table of Contents

Acknowledgements

First, we would like to thank all the people who responded to our call for essays. We appreciate the authors for being willing to share their experiences, thoughts, and for responding so well to our edits. We thank Michigan State University (MSU) Libraries for supporting us in this endeavor. The MSU Libraries' writing group was invaluable for their feedback on the initial proposal. Thanks to Library Juice Press for their encouragement and seeing value in publishing a book on this topic. We are grateful for the people in our lives, personally and professionally, who encouraged us to be where we are today. Finally, we would like to also acknowledge the enjoyment we had working together on this project and our appreciation for what we've learned from each other during the process. Each person brought different strengths that made this a better book overall.

Introduction

Jenny Brandon, who works with primarily men as a web designer, and primarily women as a reference librarian, developed the original idea for this book. When starting in her position as a library web designer, she appreciated having two of her male co-workers go out of their way to teach her about version control, how to access servers, and more. They were kind and patient, and without their help, she would have felt as if she were drowning in a world where she did not belong. Even though they were very helpful, she felt awkward, deficient in some way, and would not ask for help unless she had fully exhausted her ability to find an answer, hoping not to be viewed as incompetent or unintelligent. She was not sure if this was because she was a woman, because she lacked the traditional IT education and training, or because she was a librarian.

Jenny did not think of herself as a woman in a man's profession, but rather as a librarian with no formal IT training, working with people with computer degrees, mostly men. She was curious to find out if other women in library IT had similar experiences and thoughts. Conferring with colleagues at Michigan State University Libraries about gathering essays on the topic for a book, she found two who were also interested: Kelly Sattler, Head of Web Services, and Sharon Ladenson, Gender and Communication Studies Librarian. While the three of us share a strong interest in investigating the experiences of women in library IT, we have distinct ideas and perspectives on the topic, and, consequently, have learned from each other as well as from our contributors.

We began our process of collecting personal narratives by putting out a call on several listservs, soliciting essays about what it is like to be a woman, or working with women, in library IT. For the purposes of this collection, we considered library IT to include responsibilities in computer networks, hardware, and software support; computer programming (e.g. coding in python, php, java); web development (e.g. admins, coders, front/back end developers); and/or the management of such areas. Suggested topics included the following:

- How you started in library IT
- Stories related to being a woman in library IT
- Experiences of acceptance or resistance within the library IT community
- Tips and advice for other women seeking a career in library IT
- Changes in your career path because of entering library IT
- Changes you'd like to see happen within the library IT culture
- Advice for library management on how to improve library IT culture
- A vision for the future about/for women in library IT

We received essays covering diverse topics which bring the voices of women in library IT from the margins to the center. Contributors with varied levels of experience discuss their career trajectories, exploring how their jobs and responsibilities have evolved, changed, and grown. Reflecting on their careers, several authors also share advice for women who pursue positions in library IT. Other essays offer advice for library managers on cultivating an inclusive and productive environment. As some contributors have experienced gender bias and discrimination, they share challenges and personal strategies for countering sexism in the workplace. Developing confidence in library IT positions can also present distinct challenges for women. Several authors discuss the concept of imposter syndrome and explore how they have gradually become more comfortable in their roles (including in management positions).

Although most essays touch on more than one of these areas, we have chosen to organize them into sections based on what we feel is a primary focus, or a topic that is worth emphasizing. The sections are: advice, observations, career path, challenges, and change agents. The advice section provides guidance and tips for moving forward in the world of library IT. The observations section includes personal reflections on working in the field, as well as essays on varying topics, such as the impact of gender stereotypes on library IT. Career path essays focus primarily on the occupational trajectories of our contributors, including how our authors initially started, developed, and flourished in the field. Essays in the challenges section focus on various obstacles encountered by our authors, including sexism and unconscious bias. Finally, the change agents section includes essays with especially empowering messages and strategies for improving and transforming library IT culture. Each essay is also labelled with various tags (many supplied by our authors) to illustrate additional themes of focus.

As editors, we struggled at times during the process of reviewing essays. We discussed how dominant social and cultural expectations could potentially influence the perceptions of some of our contributors as well as reader responses to some of the essays. For example, at times we experienced some discomfort when our women contributors expressed anger in their writing. We were concerned that female anger would potentially be simply dismissed by some readers as ranting. However, we also raised questions

3

about whether we would have the same concerns if anger were expressed by men. We also wrestled with respecting and honoring the voices of our authors, while also encouraging some of them to express more confidence and less self-doubt in their narratives.

As might be expected, the majority of the authors are women. However, two men contributed; one by himself and one with women co-authors. While most of the contributors work in academic libraries, we have three contributors from public libraries. Also, not everyone has worked at the same institution their entire career. Many worked in a corporate or a non-library IT unit at some point in their careers as well. Our contributors are primarily from the United States; however, we have one author from Nigeria. The most varied demographic is a contributor's title or position they hold in their organization. We received essays from library administrators, including a vice president and a dean, as well as from several unit heads and managers. There were also diverse contributions from web developers and system librarians, catalogers, emerging technology librarians, consultants, and a system programmer. We appreciated seeing and hearing from a wide spectrum of representatives of varying roles in the library IT realm.

The world of IT also has a variety of roles and positions, which are largely held by men. Women's participation in computing-related fields has declined since the 1980s,[1] and evidence of this trend continues. According to the American Association of University Women, female participation in computing-related fields decreased from over a third of workers in 1990 to a little over a quarter in 2013.[2] Furthermore, in 2015,

---

1 Janet Abbate, "Introduction: Rediscovering Women's History in Computing," in *Women's Changing Participation in Computing* (Cambridge: MIT Press, 2012), 2.

2 Christianne Corbett and Catherine Hill, *Solving the Equation: The Variables for Women's Success in Engineering and Computing* (Washington, DC: American Association of University Women, March 2015), 8.

women occupied only 25 percent of all computing-related jobs.[3] The numbers have been especially low for women of color: Latina and African American women held only 1 and 3 percent, respectively, of computing-related jobs during that time.[4] This trend has been partially shaped by gender stratification in education. The number of women graduating with computer science degrees has been decreasing since its peak in the mid-1980s.[5] Margolis and Fisher assert that a wide variety of external factors have influenced this trend in education:

> *"By the time they finish college, most women studying computer science have faced a technical culture whose values do not match their own and have encountered a variety of discouraging experiences with teachers, peers, and curriculum. Many end up doubting their basic intelligence and their fitness to pursue computing."*[6]

3   Catherine Ashcraft, Brad McLain, and Elizabeth Eger, *Women in Tech: The Facts* (Boulder, CO: National Center for Women and Information Technology, 2016), 2, accessed December 2017, https://www.ncwit.org/sites/default/files/resources/ncwit_women-in-it_2016-full-report_final-web06012016.pdf.

4   Ibid, 2. For more information on the underrepresentation of women in IT, see William Aspray, *Women and Underrepresented Minorities in Computing: A Historical and Social Study* (Cham, Switzerland: Springer International Publishing, 2016); and Caroline Simard et al., *Climbing the Technical Ladder: Obstacles and Solutions for Mid-Level Women in Technology* (Michelle R. Clayman Institute for Gender Research and Anita Borgman Institute for Women in Technology, 2013), accessed December 2017, http://www.gedcouncil.org/sites/default/files/Climbing_the_Technical_Ladder.pdf.

5   "Degrees in Computer and Information Sciences Conferred by Degree-Granting Institutions, by Level of Degree and Sex of Student: 1970-71 through 2014-15," table 325.35, *Digest of Education Statistics*, National Center for Education Statistics, accessed December 2017, https://nces.ed.gov/programs/digest/d16/tables/dt16_325.35.asp.

6   Jane Margolis and Allan Fisher, "Introduction: Women out of the Loop," in *Unlocking the Clubhouse: Women in Computing* (Cambridge: MIT Press, 2002), 4-5.

As computers became a primary tool of the information age, they had a dramatic effect on libraries and the curation of knowledge. Librarianship is a profession dominated by women, at least in modern history. This collision of IT and libraries began to surface in the 1980s and 1990s.[7] Although automation of routine library work began previously, the personal computer as a tool for accessing information began a paradigm shift for how librarians curated and made information available. Thus, the "marriage" of libraries with IT.

A few of the contributors who worked in libraries during this time give first hand stories of their experiences taking on tasks and roles using new technologies. Those with no formal education or training, but with a natural aptitude for learning and understanding new technologies, accepted new challenges and can be credited with helping to launch the integration of computers and libraries. Yet, some of the contributors entered into library IT with a formal education and/or training in computer technologies.

Despite the proliferation of technology in libraries, relatively little has been written about women in library IT. Hildenbrand[8] has discussed the impact of library and information science education on gender inequality in library technology and management positions. Also exploring gender issues, Harris[9] conducted a study to investigate the impact of new technologies on the work of female and male employees at public and academic libraries, and found some

---

7   Clifford Lynch, "From Automation to Transformation: Forty Years of Libraries and Information Technology in Higher Education," *EDUCAUSE review* 35, no. 1 (January/February 2000): 63-64.

8   Suzanne Hildenbrand, "The Information Age versus Gender Equality? Technology and Values in Education for Library and Information Science," *Library Trends* 47, no. 4 (1999): 669-685.

9   Roma M. Harris, "Gender and Technology Relations in Librarianship," *Journal of Education for Library and Information Science* 40, no. 4 (Fall 1999): 236.

distinct gender differences. For example, while 41 percent of men interviewed felt that they had strong influence on how emerging technologies were incorporated into the workplace, only 14 percent of women shared that view. Further highlighting gender inequality in library IT, Lamont[10] reviewed statistics from the Association of Research Libraries (ARL) which showed that more men than women occupied positions as computer systems department heads. In addition, female systems department heads with more years of experience earned less than their male counterparts. Ricigliano and Houston[11] also reviewed ARL statistics, and found that men increasingly occupied technology positions, particularly in large university libraries. Gender stratification has also been evident in library IT publications. Reviewing article citations in selected library IT journals, Lamont found that men have published at much higher rates than women.[12] Moving forward, Lamont advocates for transforming organizational culture in libraries to become more inclusive, and expanding the ways we define IT.[13]

If you are looking for ways to connect with women in library IT, we would like to make you aware of opportunities, groups, conferences and other ways that people have been communicating with each other. First, the Library and Information Technology Association (LITA), is bringing technically minded people together, both women and men. Within LITA, a Women in Information Technology Interest

---

10   Melissa Lamont, "Gender, Technology, and Libraries," *Information Technology and Libraries* 28, no. 3 (September 2009): 137.

11   Lori Ricigliano and Renée Houston, "Men's Work, Women's Work: The Social Shaping of Technology in Academic Libraries," paper presented at the Association of College and Research Libraries Eleventh National Conference, Charlotte, North Carolina, April 10-13, 2003, accessed December 2017, http://www.ala.org/acrl/sites/ala.org.acrl/files/content/conferences/pdf/ricigliano.PDF.

12   Lamont, "Gender, Technology, and Libraries," 138.

13   Ibid, 141.

Group[14] has a mailing list.[15] They also put on an AvramCamp preconference at the 2017 American Library Association (ALA) Annual based on the AdaCamp model.[16] Even though it has passed, you may be inspired to either look for one locally or put on such an unconference in your own area.

There is also the LibTechWomen group, as referenced by one of our authors, Becky Yoose. LibTechWomen is a supportive space for women and their friends to network, develop skills, build confidence, and lead positive change. They offer a monthly chat on IRC with the hashtag, #libtechwomen and have a Slack group. They also hold meetups at various conferences such as Code4Lib, ALA and ACRL. See their site at libtechwomen.org to find all their social media options.

We want to thank all the contributors who worked tirelessly with us throughout the process of creating this book. We appreciate their willingness to candidly share their varied experiences, challenges, triumphs, and advice. While you may or may not agree with all they have to say, keep in mind that these essays are primarily first-hand accounts and opinions held by the authors. We hope that these narratives will generate substantive discussion and improvements in library IT.

---

14 "Women in Information Technology," *Library and Information Technology Association*, accessed December 2017, http://www.ala.org/lita/about/igs/women-in-information-technology/lit-igwiit.

15 "LITA Women in Information Technology Interest Group," *Library and Information Technology Association*, accessed December 2017, http://lists.ala.org/sympa/info/lita-women-in-tech.

16 "LITA AvramCamp Preconference at the 2017 ALA Annual Conference in Chicago," *Library and Information Technology Association* (blog), accessed December 2017, http://litablog.org/2017/03/lita-adacamp-preconference-at-the-2017-ala-annual-conference-in-chicago/.

#Advice

BE COMPETENT, BE CONFIDENT, AND DARE GREATLY: LESSONS LEARNED FROM TWENTY-FIVE YEARS OF SURVIVING AND THRIVING IN LIBRARY IT

Janet Crum

#Advice #Confidence #Opportunities #Sexism

I started my first professional librarian position twenty-five years ago, and I just celebrated my fiftieth birthday. These twin milestones have led to a good bit of reflection, as well as the usual maudlin laments about how fast the time goes and <insert cliché here>. In this brief essay, I will skip the clichés (well, mostly) and instead share some of the lessons I learned from a quarter century as a woman working, managing, and leading in library IT.

My first professional position was not in IT—it was half reference and half cataloging at a two-year college in a small town three time zones from anywhere I had ever lived. I arrived on campus in July, 1992, and the campus Internet connection arrived two months later. Thanks to an independent study experience in library school, I was one of about four people on campus who had even heard of the Internet. So within a few months, my position had expanded unofficially to include IT, and I had found my professional calling. From that experience comes the first lesson I learned: Be an opportunist. Is there something new happening in your organization that interests you? Volunteer for it! Sometimes you can be an instant expert because you know three more facts about the new thing than anyone else does. Sometimes you can teach yourself what you need to know when you need to know it. Sometimes being willing to volunteer for something outside your usual responsibilities can lead to interesting and bizarre opportunities—like a twenty-six-year-old rookie professional teaching the college president how to use email.

Which brings me to my next piece of advice: Be confident—or at least fake it. I won't say I wasn't nervous about having the college president in my email workshop—I'd be lying—but I didn't overthink it. I knew what I was talking about, so I just got on with it. That same confidence has led me to say, "Yes," to all sorts of opportunities that, had I actually thought about the possible consequences and my own limitations, would have terrified me: managing a big project, giving a keynote presentation at a conference, and becoming a library director, to name just a few. I dislike gender-based generalizations, but one rings true for me at least some of the time: Men are (in general) more likely to overestimate their abilities, while women are (in general) more likely to underestimate theirs. In my observation, this tendency helps men get more opportunities, because they are more willing to ask for them and to say, "Yes," when opportunities arise. Their confidence pays off—literally.

I can hear the protests already: "But you can't just decide to be confident!" True, but you can decide to fake it, and you can decide to take a leap of faith and say, "Yes," to something out of your comfort zone. I had two big professional epiphanies in my early years. The first happened when I recognized myself in an article about gifted women and imposter syndrome. The thesis of the article is that even highly gifted women feel like they are faking it and dread the moment when everyone will find out they are frauds. The second epiphany came when I attended a workshop on PC hardware. We spent a day taking apart a desktop computer and putting it back together. Until that time, the most I had done with hardware was to stare squiggle-eyed at the complexity of a computer's innards. The most valuable lesson I learned from that workshop had nothing to do with installing a motherboard. I learned that working with computer hardware was not some magical, mysterious black art that could be understood only by an elite group of super-geniuses; it was a skill I could learn. And if that was true of computer hardware, it was probably true of all sorts of other complicated-sounding stuff. Whenever I am faced with some complex new thing, I remember the rush of excitement I felt during that workshop when I realized that I could learn how to do something I thought was beyond me. I also remember that even some of the smartest, most capable women think they are phonies. In other words, fear is normal, and you can learn what you need to know. So say, "Yes," to opportunities that scare you and fake the confidence till you learn enough to have the real thing. That's how you grow, professionally and personally.

Now that I have spent a paragraph telling you to say, "Yes," I am going to suggest you also learn how to say, "No." I was promoted to management when my son was two years old, and three members of my immediate family had (and have) chronic medical conditions. Neither IT culture nor library management are known for valuing work-life balance. But I could not and still cannot work sixty hours a week, and I have to take time off for lots of medical appointments. So I had a frank talk with my director about expected working hours. Thankfully he was more interested in results than butt-in-seat time, so I said, "Yes," to the promotion, and a new phase of my career was born. To get those results—without the 60-hour weeks—I am strategic about how I spend my time, and I prioritize ruthlessly. For each new task, here are the questions I ask myself, along with some advice:

• Does this task need to be done at all? What purpose does it serve? Push back on work that does not add value.

- Should I be doing this? If not, who should? Learn to delegate effectively, and resist getting stuck with all the "office mom" tasks (organizing potlucks) and clerical duties (minute-taking) that often get assigned to women. Do your share, but don't do everyone else's share.

- Does this task have to be done well? I cannot do A+ work on everything. Sometimes good enough is, well, good enough. Don't waste time perfecting something that isn't important enough to warrant the effort. Just get it done.

But, you say, women are punished for advocating for themselves and for saying, "No." Well… sometimes. So let's talk about the elephant in the room: sexism. First, two caveats. I will discuss

- Personal strategies, not ways to eliminate systemic sexism.
- Strategies that have worked for me, a white, middle-class, heterosexual, cis-gendered woman. Women who do not fit that mold may struggle much more than I have and may need to adopt different approaches.

Sexism exists—in librarianship, in IT, in the world—but I usually deal with it by pretending it doesn't exist. I am neither oblivious nor stupid, and I have experienced sexism, both professionally and personally. But I get to choose (in part) how much power to give other people's prejudices. I choose to focus on doing good work and building strong relationships with colleagues, not analyzing every interaction or worrying about whether my gender will limit me. I walk into a conference room with campus IT staff—where I'm often the only woman in the room—and act like I belong there (because I do), like I am capable (because I am), and like I will be treated as a respected colleague (because I almost always will be). I find that most people take their cues from my behavior and respond to the expectations I set. This approach even worked when I was a 25-year-old rookie in a place where sexism was standard operating procedure. I had to work a little harder to be taken seriously than I do now—and I had to fend off the occasional attempt at flirting—but I was treated with respect even by senior male faculty who had reputations for being sexist.

Here are a few other lessons I have learned in dealing with sexism, both at work and in my personal life:

- Don't let fear of sexism limit you more than actual sexism does. Advocate for yourself. Say no. Ask for a raise or a promotion. Wayne Gretzky was right: you miss 100% of the shots you don't take.

- Pick your battles. You have limited time, energy, and political capital, so save them for the issues that will have the biggest impact.

- You cannot choose how other people treat you, but you can choose how much power you give them. You don't have to give every microaggression space in your head.

- Assume positive intent. Assume your co-workers will treat you as the capable professional you are. Assume the sexist comment was based on ignorance rather than malevolence and call it out accordingly ("Here's my concern about what you said," rather than, "You sexist !@#$%.") Your assumptions won't always be correct, but you will be much healthier and happier than you will be if you assume the worst in every person or situation.

I started this essay with no theme in mind other than reflecting on what I have learned in my quarter-century of library IT work. Now, though, I see a theme emerge, which I hope readers will take to heart: build your career on your terms. You don't have to limit yourself based on other people's expectations and biases. Advocate for yourself and your skills, take risks, keep learning, lift others up with you, fight the important fights, and make choices based on *your* values, not someone else's. I have built a successful career this way, and I have had a great time doing it. I hope you do too.

SUPPORT FOR WOMEN IN IT IS SUPPORT FOR THE TEAM

Allison Deluca

#Advice #SupportWomeninIT #TeamSupport

In my own experience, I've found that IT departments are particularly easy targets for antagonism. There are widespread feelings of distrust and doubt from non IT library employees towards their IT departments. Part of this is because IT runs in the background of every company, only becoming visible when something goes wrong, and inevitably, something will go wrong.

There seems to be an unwritten expectation that all IT professionals have knowledge of everything IT related (except when you're a woman!). This happens in all levels of an organization. Administration is not immune to these assumptions and may even perpetuate these views among workers in their organization. This is akin to asking a businessman to know everything there is to know within the business world, from accounting to marketing, from law to human resources policy. As a woman this script is flipped–others will assume you don't know what you're talking about no matter what the circumstances. My own experiences in IT have been mostly positive, but those difficult and negative experiences are not easily erased from memory. I've had some of my most difficult interactions in my career while trying to fix problems for my colleagues. Some of those experiences make up my everyday office reality. Imagine your colleagues conveying the assumption that you could not possibly understand the very basics of your job when you ask for help in any particular situation. I have, at times, detailed every step taken while troubleshooting, only to have everything I had already done relayed to me all over again. I cannot say definitively this is because I am a woman in IT, but I cannot rule out gender bias.

The IT department is not only critical to your libraries' success, but also to your organization's harmony. Your IT department is the backbone of your library. Technology, in all its forms, is no longer separate from library culture and your IT department is uniquely qualified to support the library in more ways than you can count.

Ways to Support Your IT Department

Support from administration begins by never being the source of animosity towards anyone in your IT department. Show respect for your staff and treat them the same way you would like to be treated. I've personally sat through meetings where IT matters are discussed, and watched administrators roll their eyes when they are told the opposite of what they wanted to hear. I've had colleagues tell me they've borne the brunt of someone's anger over something as trivial as a mouse not working. The frustrations of working with technology can overwhelm some people, but no one should feel they are able to treat me or someone else as a punching bag for their frustrations. This means that if you do hear of your staff members being treated poorly, the proper action should be taken to ensure it doesn't happen again. Of course, never be the person treating your staff poorly.

Denounce undue criticism from co-workers and staff and never be the one to set a poor example. In the course of everyday conversations, co-workers sometimes vent about their peers and working conditions. Denouncing criticism is an effective way to show your staff you appreciate everything they do. If you notice the criticism is particularly strong or seems to be only pointed when it comes to the women in your IT department, make sure your staff knows it will not be tolerated.

Try your best to fund continuing education requests from your IT staff. As we all know, the IT world moves at a pace much faster than that of the library world. Staying up-to-date is always in the back of the mind of your staff, given the constant threat of outsourcing and obsolescence. The IT field changes at such a rapid pace that it is vital that management understands the pressures of being in the field. Find money in your budget to help them take courses, attend conferences, or get new certifications. If funding in your library is low, at least acknowledge that you understand how important it is for them to keep up their skills. My own continuing education helped me to secure the position I am in right now. My supervisor, at the time, encouraged me to take computer science courses and luckily, the management at our library was supportive.

Appreciate efforts of IT staff for handling both successful and unsuccessful projects. Sometimes things can be unpredictable, and, consequently, things may take longer than expected.

Support the decisions IT staff make for your library. From time to time you may find yourself questioning their recommendations when you ask for their help. However, while you may understand the first two or three reasons why something will work, your staff may know another 20 reasons why it won't work.

Address communication barriers head on. Communication barriers happen at all levels of any organization, but there is another layer of misunderstanding that enters when discussing all things technical. There may be times when you cannot understand anything your Server Admin is saying. And there may be times when he or she just cannot explain something to you in layman's terms. I can recall more than one instance when taking computer science courses where my instructor would do their best to explain a new concept to the class only to be met with 40 blank stares.

Everyone's experiences working in IT will be defined by the organizational culture at that library, but, there are many steps that administration can take to ensure those experiences are positive. The women in your IT department may have different experiences than the men in your department, but support and understanding will solidify confidence for all in the field.

A Road Not Planned: My Journey in Library IT

Denise A. Garofalo

#Advice #CareerPath #Challenges

My path into library IT was not really a planned journey. Although my mentor kept telling me, "Computers, Denise. The future is in computers!" and I kept that advice in the back of my mind, my college courses were in English and History, based on guidance from an advisor who seemed to believe those areas were logical for someone going into library work. Did gender play a role in my advisor's counseling? Perhaps, but at the time I was naïve and overwhelmed with all the possibilities that college presented, and welcomed advice from someone who seemed more "in the know." Once in library school, my studies were broad to support a generalist position. After what seemed like hundreds of resume mailings and dozens of interviews, I was hired as a cataloger for a public library in another state.

My cataloging duties expanded into acquisitions; I was not hesitant to answer the phone to speak with salespeople, unlike some of my coworkers. My supervisor decided my telephone skills were the right fit for another new responsibility—transmitting the library's orders electronically, my first foray into library IT. In the eyes of my supervisor, I became the library's tech person overnight by successfully submitting and printing orders which involved fiddling with the phone handset and adjusting the printer and multipart order form).

There was a male librarian on staff (hired at the same time as I) who was nominally the "tech whiz." He received that designation due to his gender and the misconception that he must have technology knowledge. The reality was that he was not comfortable with anything beyond his Apple computer. I must say I resented that he was initially seen by most of the library staff as the go-to tech support person based not on his ability but on his gender, while I was the one who was actually doing tech support for the library, albeit just in my department. However, once staff realized that his tech skills were superficial and limited, they started to look elsewhere. Soon library staff were coming to me to resolve all of what they considered their technology-related issues. Terminal display not working? Call Denise. Security door not working right? Call Denise. Having trouble replacing the correction ribbon in the public typewriter? Call Denise. The list just grew and grew. I soon realized that a willingness to work over the phone with a tech support person was my most useful library IT skill.

When the library administration decided to begin purchasing videos, I added audiovisual support to my library IT task list—mending broken videocassette cases, splicing videotape, and doing any other VHS repairs needed to keep the collection vibrant and in circulating condition. I began representing the library at IT-related meetings, where I started networking with people who were dealing with similar issues. This led me to develop a list of resource people to consult when I had questions I couldn't answer about topics such as wiring and cabling, suggestions for furniture for public access equipment, and/or recommendations for catalog card printing software.

My next library position acknowledged my library IT skills, as my title was Head of Technical Services and Automated Systems. My new library director told me that my demonstrated library IT skills substantially influenced my selection for this position. My library IT responsibilities focused around our integrated library management system (ILMS). The library had just joined an ILMS consortia. Consequently, barcoding the library's collection, converting records into MARC, and subsequently loading records into the system became my primary focus. Since we were using a vendor for the retrospective conversion, my duties mostly involved training staff and temporary workers to barcode materials and use the ILMS, plus some oversight. Once the project finished, I left the position due to my marriage and relocation.

Fortunately, I was able to land a newly created library IT job at a state library. I created a regional cataloging center, assisting libraries in acquiring library technology, helping them prepare for a regionally-based ILMS, and providing training in various library IT aspects. In order to perform my job responsibilities, I needed to become proficient in the UNIX operating system, which I did by teaching myself from books.

I continued to cultivate my network of library IT contacts. Having friends working through similar bureaucratic mazes, dealing with comparable hurdles, and sharing tales was very supportive. We would share our frustrations and challenges, particularly about perceptions and respect. I asked my network why, if my male colleague and I visited a site, did they approach my colleague and seek his advice yet treat me as his assistant? I was less assertive then, actually rather shy, and my network suggested I walk into a site in front of this colleague, so the site staff would see me first, and that I speak up and do the introductions and make myself more visible right from the start. Their advice was spot on, and at some sites I did see a change in their attitude towards my technical capability. I hesitated to label these actions and mindsets gender bias, but that's what it was. My network had provided me with a non-confrontational method to deal with those situations. When my husband's job situation necessitated a move to another state, I was saddened to leave. Fortunately, I did have my library IT network to mine in my search for a new position.

My network provided fruitful information and contacts, and I again found myself offered a newly-created position to bring library automation to a multi-county library system. I oversaw installing an ILMS, encouraging system member participation, and training member staff in using the ILMS. This library IT venture required a level of networking and telecommunications knowledge that I did not possess. I began reading and attending workshops on digital telecom and TCP/IP and learned how to solder terminal connections, run data cable, and perform telecom tests.

After a change in employment for a few years, I've returned to library IT as a systems librarian at an academic library (a tenure-track position). My responsibilities encompass library IT and technical services, reference duties, collection development, instruction, web development, and liaison areas. I also serve as the library's point person for interactions with campus IT.

I meet monthly with the campus CIO and the IT Technical Services Director. These meetings are very beneficial. I address outstanding concerns, we discuss upcoming projects and proposals, and keep communication open and flowing. I am the library's IT interface, serving as the funnel through which any IT difficulties, glitches, or troubles are reported.

Discussing library IT with the campus IT folks is very helpful. They assist me with dealing with our ILMS vendor on difficulties (e.g., printing snags, updating the ILMS servers' OS, acquiring security certificates, etc.). When the library moved to a new building, campus IT assisted with the physical relocation of the library's servers.

I have been fortunate that my experiences in library IT overall have been so positive. Being the lone woman or one of few women at IT-related gatherings hasn't impeded my ability to have my voice be heard and contribute to discussions and planning, especially as I have grown more confident in my skills. Perhaps my interests in science fiction, sports (Go Mets!), and gaming provided me with an "in" to the male-dominated information technology world. With one particular group of male IT workers, I was experiencing difficulty in having service requests handled in a timely fashion. One day while waiting in the tech support office, I spied a screensaver with images of a particular video game. I then mentioned how I played that game, too, and asked their opinion of the game's ending. All of a sudden the gruffness and evasiveness disappeared, and we had a great discussion about that game and others, with tech support troubleshooting questions directed at me sprinkled in the mix. I answered those and gave some right back at them. After that exchange, my interactions with these tech support guys became much less forced and belligerent. I have found if you can demonstrate that you really are the IT professional you say you are, and perhaps find some common interest, then any hint of being an outsider fades away.

Any woman pursuing a position in IT should be prepared to encounter some skepticism from male colleagues. Don't let their prejudices and bad attitudes get you down! Show them you deserve to be in IT just as much as they do. Be willing to work and demonstrate that your skills, knowledge, and outlook make you a proficient and capable IT professional.

My advice remains the same for library IT: be prepared to show them you are rightfully the library IT person for your organization. Speak up and make your voice heard. Don't let negative attitudes hold you back.

Try to cultivate a mentor. This more experienced or more knowledgeable person can help guide you and provide you with welcome counsel, suggesting alternatives when you encounter obstacles or adversaries. Mentors are trusted advisors who are always in your corner. They can provide a fresh perspective on a situation and can recommend different ways to reach your goals. Think of a mentor as a guide who is trying to ensure you get to your destination with as few detours as possible.

Along with a mentor, develop a network of peers, other people working in library IT. Attend conferences, workshops, and trainings. These are effective avenues to meet others in similar positions. There are library listservs and organizations focused on library IT: join them. For instance, LITA (Library Information Technology Association, a division of ALA) and WEB4LIB. Reach out to your neighboring library IT colleagues. You may need to do some footwork and look them up on their institution's website, but once you've made the connection, you will be glad you did. You can consult with those in your network when you seek recommendations for vendors, want to know how they implemented a particular technology, or you have a question only their expertise will address. Your network can also be useful when you are seeking a job change. They may know about prospective employers, job openings, or people in your potential new organization. You may also consider contacting members of your network to provide you with a reference.

My hope and vision for the future is that any prejudices or preconceived notions people may have about women in IT or library IT will disappear. Gender should never be related to capability when it comes to perceptions about IT or any field. Women already working in library IT can help create inclusive and supportive work environments. We can't eliminate the gender imbalance, but we can work towards eliminating the lack of gender diversity in IT through our actions, such as becoming a mentor to young women in school, thereby showing them that they too can work in IT and have an exciting and challenging career.

My Journey and Tips for Women Interested in IT

Vincci Kwong

#Advice #Challenges #Tips

My name is Vincci Kwong, Head of Library Web Services at Franklin D. Schurz Library at Indiana University South Bend. My journey of getting involved in information technology started when I took my first Pascal programming class in high school. Since then I learned about different programming languages like C++, Java, JavaScript, CGI, ASP, PHP and SQL during my undergraduate studies for my BS in Information Technology. Based on my programming experience, I found that once you have mastered a programming language, it is pretty easy to adapt to a different programming language. When learning a new programming language, I find it helpful to review examples. One of the websites I often find helpful if I need to look up a quick reference is w3schools.com. If you are a visual learner, YouTube, Khan Academy and Lynda.com are great resources.

My personal experience as a woman working in a male-dominated IT field is pretty positive. Administrators and colleagues have recognized and appreciated my capabilities. Even though everyone is generally supportive, I have encountered trust issues on a few occasions. In meetings, I have presented information which my colleagues seemed to doubt. However, they accepted the same information when presented by a male counterpart. An example was when I worked on a reference statistics program. A few years ago, the reference department was interested in implementing a program to track usage statistics for reference services. Being aware of a home-grown reference statistics program from another institution, I adapted and revised the program based on the needs of the reference department. The revised program provided an online portal for the reference department to gather statistics based on different types of reference questions. During the testing phase, a few of the reference librarians agreed the system met the need for tracking service usage. Unfortunately, the program wasn't implemented. A couple of years ago, a male reference librarian suggested using a third-party online web form to track reference usage statistics. The online web form was implemented as an official tool to gather reference statistics.

As web technologies keep evolving, in-depth knowledge of markup languages, like HTML and CSS, is not required for creating and maintaining websites. Content management systems and APIs enable individuals to create functional websites with minimal coding knowledge. With content management systems making publishing easier, the web services librarian can focus more on a leadership role, from providing advice on creating great content to designing user-friendly interfaces. I still recommend learning the basics of HTML and CSS as this will help with troubleshooting when issues or problems arise.

Throughout my career, I have learned a few things to share with women seeking a career in library IT:

1. Obtain Buy-In Before You Start a Project

You may have a great solution to enhance the workflow of a department. However, if you do not have buy-in, there is a good chance that your application may not fit well with the needs of the department. If the application is not implemented, not only would this process waste time and effort, but it also may undermine morale.

2. Show, Then Tell

When communicating a project idea with fellow library colleagues, try to show your ideas visually instead of using mysterious terminology. If you are redesigning a web interface, provide a mockup to illustrate the new interface. If you are bringing new tech gadgets or a new program to your library, show photos or webpages from other libraries implementing the same program or gadgets. A visual presentation provides others with a better understanding of your ideas.

3. Share Your Hidden Responsibilities

As a web developer, I often time spend many hours in debugging and patching back end systems. While these tasks are not obvious to our colleagues or users, they are nevertheless very important. Sharing back end tasks not only enables your colleagues to have a better understanding of your responsibilities, but also helps to increase appreciation and respect for your contributions.

4. Learn About Personality and Work Style

Different individuals have diverse personalities and work styles. As we work in teams, it is important to understand and learn the personalities and work styles of your colleagues. I once worked with a colleague who preferred instruction when working on projects. As a result, I provided instruction instead of having her explore and investigate solutions for a project. Accommodating different personalities and work styles helps to increase work efficiency.

5. Find a Tech Buddy

When going to meetings or conferences, watch for other IT folks. Networking with other IT folks enables you to learn areas of IT that you are not familiar with, and is also a great way to keep yourself updated with the latest technology trends. If you find someone who has similar job responsibilities, this will be an opportunity to learn from each other and share ideas.

6. Don't Be Shy, Ask for Help!

When encountering issues or problems, do not get frustrated for not being able to resolve them. Whether it is debugging or looking for a new technology solution, help is out there. Join different listservs or communities, ask your questions, and chances are there will be someone else who will be able to suggest a solution for you. So, don't be shy and ask for help!

Through my committee work, I have met and worked with women who are in administrative and leadership roles in library IT. Administrative and leadership positions held by women in library IT include, but are not limited to the following: Head, Discovery & User Experience; Director, Office of Libraries Technology; Director of Discovery Services; Director of Web Services and Emerging Technologies; Head of Design & Discovery; and Executive Director of Library Information Technology Association (LITA). These women lead a variety of IT operations in libraries serving student populations from 12,000 to 70,000. This affirms my belief that women can do IT, and I envision a growing number of women will lead the library IT community in the future.

How Two Women Embraced Their Path to IT Management

Rachel Vacek and Kat Hagedorn

#Advice #Advocacy #CareerPath #GetThingsDone
#Leadership #Management #Mentorship #UnconsciousBias

Rachel's Background

In 1999, I earned my undergraduate degree in English and wasn't sure what to do next. After graduation, I worked for a year in a bookstore and eventually decided to pursue my MLIS. Seventeen years and four positions later, I'm now working at the University of Michigan Library as the Head of Design & Discovery. I've taught courses and workshops on technology and information literacy, provided reference and desktop support, and developed many websites and applications. As I moved to new positions at different institutions, I purposefully focused on expanding my knowledge of web services, digital libraries, and user experience. When the opportunity to move into a management position opened up, I didn't feel ready for it, but I pursued it as part of my career growth. Over time I built relationships, earned trust and respect, and gained confidence. I also sought out leadership and management training opportunities, and I'm now more comfortable being a manager. I find it very rewarding to mentor and help others unlock their potential.

There were many people who saw something in me and wanted to help me on my journey. I was always thinking about the future, the big picture, and what I needed to do to help make that vision a reality. I also sought out individuals whom I thought were successful and could offer advice on how best to make an impact. Over time, I learned that although it's important to have supportive colleagues who believe in you, it's just as, if not more, important to believe in yourself.

Kat's Background

I received a biology degree from Cornell and gravitated to libraries almost immediately upon graduation. After getting my MLIS from the University of Michigan, I enjoyed a number of positions building taxonomies and metadata, which eventually led me back to U-M to be a project manager for the OAIster project and eventually the U-M digital library. With these positions, I had the opportunity to be part of overarching, strategic conversations inside of our Library IT division, and this whet my whistle for leading change as opposed to solely managing it. Along with Rachel, I didn't feel quite ready to be Head of Digital Content & Collections, but nevertheless pursued it as an opportunity for career growth. Since moving into management, I've begun learning more about my team and how to shape our efforts towards creating the best digital library experience.

Along with many women in IT, those who believed in and helped me understand my own path were primarily men. I considered them far ahead of their time in recognizing the value of someone green, a little scared of new opportunities, and very much unsure of her place in IT. At the time, I assumed that being part of IT meant that I had to be a coder. That concept has since changed dramatically to include those who develop, design, and manage, among many other roles, but in the mid

1990s this was less clear. Those who encouraged me saw I was eager to promote, preserve, and manage spaces in libraries, and particularly in IT. They helped shape my vision and taught me to rely on my instincts and experience. This has been extremely useful in my transition to management.

Unconscious Bias

Whether we like to admit it or not, bias is something that happens regularly in the workplace. It's an issue that sometimes requires us to "do battle" with male employees. While we can all get formal training on unconscious bias, our concerns center around the difficulty of changing the status quo. We can start recognizing where bias factors into our work and relationships with others, but we need something more pertinent to start changing our own habits. It's helpful to look at ourselves and identify patterns of unconscious bias that may be influencing our decision-making processes. It's also good to practice having a conscious awareness of our biases, and engage in conversations with colleagues about their successes and challenges in doing the same.

Women in IT often have an unconscious bias because of the imbalance of men in IT, and men in management positions in particular. In libraries, there are usually more women than men; however, in IT departments, men are almost always the majority. Whether following men throughout our career is a pipeline problem or a different kind of systemic problem, the end result is that we sometimes feel deficient. Like begets like, and as we continue down our paths of following men, we are showcasing it as the primary pathway for other women in the field, as well as unconsciously bolstering the concept of following in the footsteps of men. In many ways, we consider this work to be part of a "revolution." It is pushing an agenda that requires folks in the field – men and women! – to be taught, trained and have their thinking modified around the concept of unconscious bias.

What's our advice?

- Take unconscious bias training, and apply it in everything you do.
- Encourage everyone in IT to take that training, especially the men.
- Take all opportunities to showcase that training so others can begin to learn.
- Push your own team to be part of the revolution.

Women Mentors and Colleagues

An interesting counterpoint to our real-world examples of following the lead of men is the involvement of women in our professional lives. In both our situations, besides having very few female bosses, we have also had few mentors who were female. One could consider this solely a pipeline problem except that we've each had a number of women colleagues in every position we've been in. And in many cases, these women were strong, focused, passionate advocates for IT and the services and products we offered. Unfortunately, they weren't usually in management positions.

Mentorship is mostly about leadership. It's the recognition of value in another person and the intention to help shape that person's viewpoint of the landscape and current worldview of a given profession. When people move into a new position, they hope for more than just going through the standard onboarding procedures to gain a deeper understanding. We hope that our women colleagues who have been in the profession longer than we have will take time to welcome and show us the ropes, because they, too, understand and have experienced the challenges of being a woman in IT.

We recognize that there are a large number of hurdles to overcome being a woman in IT. Our female colleagues are working overtime to show their value to the organization itself. This leaves little time for outreach to new, less experienced colleagues coming into the organization. This can be threatening to some extent–if it's hard enough to show your own value, you might be reluctant to encourage another woman to show her value, too. However, the result of mentoring is a leaning, more and more, towards women having equal footing with men in this field. It may look like slight movement, but each time we mentor someone, it shifts the balance.

What's our advice?

- Be proactive about taking another female colleague's hand and helping her find her path.
- Seek out your own mentor no matter what stage you are in your career.
- Encourage men, too! It's vital we all learn how to mentor women.
- It's important that women learn how to mentor both women and men to cultivate newer models of leadership.

Leadership and Management

Often becoming a manager is not an intentional path. Positions open up, and someone who believed in us, or has recognized our leadership capabilities, encourages us to apply for that next step up. We often don't feel ready to move into management because we haven't received the training needed prior to obtaining those positions. It's up to us to find opportunities and request that training.

The title of manager doesn't necessarily mean a person is also a leader. We both have worked for exceptional managers who were also inspiring leaders, as well as managers who were less than successful at leading or coaching. We believe that it's important to not look at training as a single learning opportunity, but more as a pursuit in lifelong learning. In some environments, women may need to lead differently than they would normally in order to overcome unintentional barriers.

Managers need to continue learning management skills and how to be an effective leader in all stages of their career.

As we are both department heads and manage people, we also want to emphasize that anyone moving into positions of leadership should get training on the difference between managing people and managing projects. We embrace the *Getting Things Done*[1] philosophy which emphasizes moving your actionable work to a trusted system external from your mind so you can focus your attention on tasks and not have to worry about recalling everything. We recognize it's important to produce quality work, but management is also about leadership, and transitioning to this philosophy can be challenging if you have only been managing projects and not people.

What's our advice?

- Be persistent in learning about the differences between management and leadership, and apply what you learn.
- Learn about management and leadership topics outside your comfort zone.
- Think about how the *Getting Things Done* philosophy applies to the management of people.

Concluding Thoughts

Being a woman in IT can certainly have its challenges, as is evidenced by our thoughts about bias, mentorship, and leadership. Women can be successful in management positions and leadership roles, but they may need to work a little harder to achieve that success. If you want to move into management, think about your support network, the people you admire, and the people you recognize as allies. Do they understand how to

---

1   David Allen, *Getting Things Done: The Art of Stress-Free Productivity* (New York, NY: Penguin Books, 2015), 3-4.

navigate the biases and roadblocks you might encounter as a woman in IT? Are they willing to mentor? What kinds of training opportunities are available, and if there are none, how can you create them? Do you recognize female colleagues who can assist you, or others that might need your help? If you have the passion to make Library IT more inclusive and welcoming to women, we encourage you think about our advice as you embrace your path to management.

Finding Your Job-Career Balance

Melissa Wisner

#Advice #CareerStrategy #ProjectManagement
#VerticalNetworking

My career in academic library IT spans fifteen years, and multiple organizations. I have managed dozens of application upgrades, software implementation projects, database migrations, data conversion and reconciliation projects. I have created new product teams, forecasted five-year IT service outlooks, and established annual software development cycles. Once, while helping resolve a major technical problem, I used the first person singular to express a path towards resolution, and in response, a male colleague asked me to indicate, "Who's idea was that?"

While this is one of many personal encounters of sexist behavior in IT, the dismissal and questioning of a woman's IT abilities can also be a common experience. There will be situations, people, and outcomes, that will cause you to call into question your abilities and strengths, and the value of your contributions. By developing a strong foundation of self-awareness and professional skills, and a well-rounded peer network and career philosophy, you should be able to speak and respond with confidence, knowing there is more to your story than someone else's narrative. My best advice for women seeking a career in IT is to focus on transferable skills. Learn business analysis, project management, data querying, analysis, and visualization. These in-demand business skills are transferable to any area of IT, as well as organizations and industries with IT components. Not only are these skills core IT competences, but they will also help develop your management abilities, prioritization experience, customer service mindsets, group facilitation expertise, big-picture thinking, leadership, and influence. These areas of influence are exactly where women in IT organizations need to be represented, and have their perspectives included. In addition to this IT foundation, learn how to write and practice critical thinking. A background in the humanities will serve you well in that regard. This advice may seem in conflict with the considerable emphasis placed on the need to learn programming, followed by the question of why so few women are in computer science. That is a worthwhile examination, however, the heightened emphasis and significance placed on programming seems out of balance with the comprehensive IT needs of almost any business. Yes, libraries and other industries need programming to accomplish their work, but it is not the only means to that end. Programming is a singular aspect of the work in Libraries and IT. Even within the standard frameworks of IT, such as agile/SCRUM, the key role of the development team is not to be mistaken as consisting of only programmers. The agile/SCRUM development team is defined as "everyone and every skill required to complete the task" including testers, data specialists, and information architects. My advice is not to lose sight of this bigger picture, and your longer-term career aspirations. I have some concerns about a possibly unintended, but buried message in those social marketing campaigns, that women need to pursue programming to gain entry, or competitive advantage in IT, but by following such a singular pursuit they could miss the equally marketable, and potentially more influential opportunities in IT. My concern with this marketing blitz is a possible missed subtlety that women may now find a place doing that type of work, because sooner rather than later, programming will increasingly remain an entry level position in IT departments. Consider for example, how many IT managers and directors of IT you have worked with who also know programming. It isn't 1:1. The IT managers, directors, and chief X officers are people who can lead, analyze, and articulate the service direction a tool like programming should take. These positions are often groups of stakeholders, managing multiple business channels, including vendor and contract management, all while helping outline strategic goals and service concepts. Much of these skills will come from non-programming experiences, such as the skill sets developed through project management and business analysis roles. Successfully managing an IT department in a library, will depend on a comprehensive set of business and IT skills. For example, IT Program and Portfolio Managers will tell you that the future of IT is as much financial, as it is technical. So, while I too would encourage women of any age to pursue IT as a career, I would want to make sure my message is comprehensive regarding the range of skills, education, training, and assets a woman should consider bringing to the profession. I want to encourage women considering the field of IT to set their educational and professional objectives as high as possible. Don't aim to be someone who could get a job in IT, aim to be someone who will lead and influence IT across an organization.

The next best advice I could provide to women in IT is to recognize that your job is not your career. This is an easy misconception to make, particularly early in your career, when your primary thought will be "wanting to be good at your job" or understandably "wanting to get a job." However, your job is only a single facet of your career. I encourage you to think of your career as everything you will do as a member of your chosen profession, and not just a series of jobs you will hold. When I think of women in IT whom I admire, it is for the well-rounded careers they have managed, which includes positions held, but also their professional involvement and commitment to advance the profession and share the knowledge we generate. I was lucky that my first boss not only explained, but also demonstrated to me the value of developing this career outlook. To illustrate, think of your career like a pie chart, with this as an example:

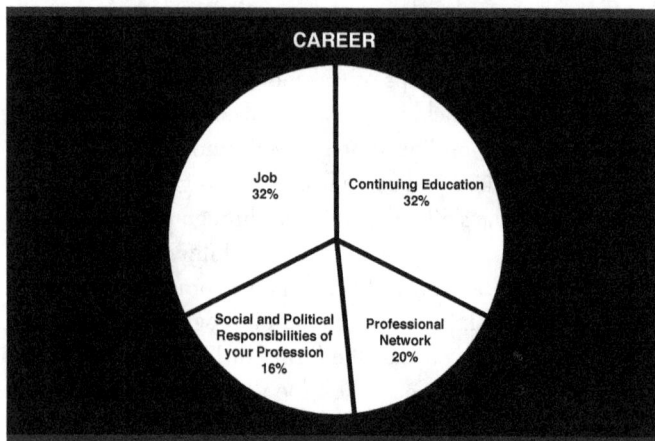

CAREER

Job 32%

Continuing Education 32%

Social and Political Responsibilities of your Profession 16%

Professional Network 20%

Determine a balance that works for your career at every stage. Earlier in your career, you might allocate more time to developing a professional network, whereas with mid-career experience, you might spend more time mentoring new colleagues, or championing the social issues of your profession with your perspective of how such matters have evolved. You may have additional areas to allocate, such as presentations and publications. This example allocation is intended to demonstrate the job-career balance women need to be mindful of, and regarding our time in this way provides us with more ownership over the direction of our careers. Some aspect of your job in IT will always be undergoing change. (This is another reason having transferable skills is strategic. Technical platforms and preferred programming languages will change, but management skills, and business analysis skills will always be needed). In any position you hold, you may not consistently receive the most strategic, or cutting-edge opportunities, but even under the most ideal working conditions you should always aspire to create those opportunities for your career. Women in IT should be as deliberate as possible about achieving their career goals. Outline what they are for yourself, be mindful about checking on your progress, and examine if how you are spending time and effort is helping you achieve those goals. In IT, as in most professions, women are sometimes measured by how "helpful" they are perceived to be around the office. Please, do be a team player. Participate equally in the primary professional tasks a team needs to accomplish for a goal. This should not include the office housework, categories of tasks that would be "helpful" for someone to get done (e.g. taking meeting minutes, reserving the meeting rooms), but are not examples of work that would become a bullet point on your resume. Remember that managing your time effectively doesn't mean you accomplish your to do list each day, rather it should be about the quality and categories of work on your to do list each day.

Another important step in managing a job-career balance for women in IT is encouraging women to see the value of networking and maintaining peer relationships with women across all stages of their careers. When you first enter the professional world of IT, you might meet and commiserate with women at the same career phase as you. However, an important aspect of moving up and planning for your career growth, is to start "thinking up" and being exposed to women who are at mid-career, or senior level status, thereby establishing a vertical network of women contacts within the IT profession. Following this approach also ensures that you will always have a steady professional circle of support throughout your career, as people enter, move-up, and retire. If you are in your mid-career, pair up young women starting out with other mid-level women. Make those introductions. This supports upward mobility within the profession. Young women two to three years into a career in digital preservation would gain advantage from being introduced to the woman who has been working as a Director of Digital Preservation for the last four years. The same Director of Digital Preservation will gain additional political savvy from having coffee with the Associate University Librarian for IT. I think any mild awkwardness around spending some work time with staff at diverse levels needs to be dissolved and we should broaden the concept of peers. Women at every stage of their IT career would benefit from forming these less typical peer networks. If, ultimately, we would like to see more women in IT, and more women being recruited into IT senior management positions, we need to start helping each other out, without the false assumption that there is only room for some of us, or if you feel you had to fight to get where you are, that any extension of help to another will weaken your footing. For women and men, it takes more than empathy, it takes acting on your intentions.

TRUST ME, I'M A LIBRARY IT PROFESSIONAL

Jingjing Wu

#Advice #Communication

The topic of women in library IT is an issue worth raising, in my opinion, because: (1) there are often fewer female IT professionals than male IT professionals in libraries; (2) life for a woman in library information technology may not be easy; and (3) with the increased use of technology in libraries, more women may be interested in becoming library IT professionals. Just as women in managerial positions may face questions regarding their personalities or capabilities, women entering the traditionally male dominated field of science and technology may face similar questions. Recent research from Robert Half UK[2] found that UK IT directors believed proving competence and challenging existing stereotypes are the greatest barriers for women working in IT. From my perspective, to break the barriers, a female IT professional should establish trust among her

2   "Proving competence and challenging stereotypes are the greatest barriers faced by women in IT," *Robert Half UK*, September 29, 2016, https://www. roberthalf.co.uk/press/proving-competence-and-challenging-stereotypes-are-greatest-barriers-faced-women-it

IT peers, non-IT colleagues, and the administration. I believe that communication is key to the path of trust.

Obtain Trust from IT Peers

In my library, we primarily have three technical teams to serve both public and internal technology needs: Public Operations, IT Support, and Application Development. As Web Librarian, I am not part of any of these three teams, but I collaborate closely with them. I consider all these technicians, engineers, and developers my IT peers. I was the only female IT person until a new developer was hired two months ago.

Shortly after I started, I suggested a web content audit to identify active pages and archive legacy files. The Application Development Team and I quickly established a workflow where I would send the list of files to be archived to them; then they would review and approve the list; finally, I would move these files to the archiving server. During the process, I became familiar with the entire website, along with the assistance of the Application Development Team. When the audit was finished, I shared the document about the active and archived files. This document is helpful for both current and new developers to understand the status of the library website. As a result, the Application Development Team became more confident with my accessing the web server independently, and assigned privileges to me for other web applications.

When I develop a new web application, I rarely start from scratch. Instead, I manage to identify similar applications, investigate the existing design ideas, then tweak them to meet the new requirements. I always strive to keep my own code clean, readable, and consistent in style. I group relevant features together, and leave descriptive comments to help both my future self and other developers understand the code. At the same time, when I read code from other web developers, it is an enjoyable experience for me if the code has been written elegantly and commented well. For IT professionals, procedures and documents are helpful communication tools in keeping best practices, ensuring quality work, getting newcomers started quickly, sharpening skills through others' experience, and building trust among team members.

Obtain Trust from non-IT Colleagues

Primarily, the IT department serves a supporting role in a library, whether the work involves computer network configuration and maintenance, hardware/software support, programming, or web development. It is common for a library IT professional to commit her/his time and skills to facilitate non-IT colleagues' work or collaborate with other departments to make their services more accessible to end users. Listening to non-IT colleagues' expectations and understanding their needs provides a sound foundation for deeper communication.

Once a colleague who volunteered to develop a website for a professional committee came to me for help. With knowledge of HTML, she had already designed the layout of the site and prepared the content. But she did not know Cascading Style Sheets (CSS) and the content management system well. Over the phone, I walked her through the features of the content management system she was not familiar with, and messaged her basic CSS code to implement her design. I advised then if she were interested in learning more about CSS, I would be ready to demonstrate. Later, in my office, I showed her how to find the style information of a web page using Chrome DevTools, as well as some intermediate CSS code and resources to quickly find advanced CSS code. With these skills, she has been more capable of making her design a reality. I would like my non-IT colleagues to come to me with more advanced questions, which would expand my horizons and enhance the computer literacy of my non-IT colleagues.

When I am not able to provide a solution instantly, I explain the technical deadlock, suggest a workaround, and offer to respond later. My non-IT colleagues then comprehend technologies and my work better. Meanwhile, I gain their trust as well as appreciation.

Obtain Trust from the Administration

Not all library directors or deans have an in-depth knowledge of technology, and yet they are the final decision makers when acquiring new technologies. Typically, IT professionals offer advice to the library administration on equipment/system selection. When offering suggestions, IT professionals would present evidence, make comparisons, and explain the pros and cons to help the administration make informed decisions. Gradually, library IT professionals build trust with the administration.

Summary

Communication is as critical to those who work in IT as it is to most other professionals. In this regard, IT positions are not as different as outsiders might imagine. Women who are interested in taking on responsibilities as library IT professionals should be able to accomplish this with proper training. In most cases, knowledge and technical competence make IT professionals more confident, persuasive and trustworthy in their communication with others. This is why as an IT professional, I believe in life-long learning. Along with developing communication skills, keeping my knowledge and technical skills fresh is the magic weapon to winning trust among my IT peers, non-IT colleagues, and the administration.

#Observations

Librarian as CIO? Naturally!

Susie Speer Corbett

#Observations #CareerPath #LibrarianAsCIO
#ManagementAdvice #NotJustaLibrarian #RedefineLibrarian
#UnLimited

Background

My career as a female librarian working in IT began in 1981. The IBM PC had just been introduced in August that year, and I graduated library school that same month. Since then, I have done all sorts of things: taken PCs apart and added hard drives or memory; set up barcode readers, receipt printers and self-checkout stations; implemented the first Novell network in our library; ran integrated library systems; and managed teams providing IT support for the organization. I have managed IT within a library and for the library's parent organization.

As the new century rolled in, I worked at the Wake Area Health Education Center (Wake AHEC), as the Director of Information Resources, managing the library, a conference center and IT for the AHEC. Though our positions were funded by the statewide AHEC, we were employees of the hospital to which we were attached. In addition to my groups, our AHEC included nine clinical practices, and the continuing education team. My IT team worked on the "bleeding edge." We implemented a thin-client solution for the clinics so they could easily run a patient scheduling and payment system at a cheaper cost than other areas of the hospital.[1] We put together a consortium of three AHEC libraries to run the Dynix Horizon integrated library system (ILS). I made sure my IT team was focused on customer service. They would frequently start their day by walking through the building proactively asking clients if things were working ok.

Though we were tightly affiliated with the hospital, our work and therefore our IT needs were much different from normal hospital IT needs. When I purchased a server, I didn't need it to be up 24x7 with RAID and all kinds of built-in redundancies. This didn't sit well with hospital IT. It was in this role that I found the most resistance from others in IT. I was told that one of the chief IT people in the hospital, someone we had to work closely with, referred to me as "just a f*ing librarian." This attitude made it difficult to work with them on projects like piggy-backing on their Help Desk for our clients and putting our servers in their server rooms. We had the luxury of being a small team with a small, well-defined set of clients, while they had to manage the security and computing for the 5,000 plus clients in the hospital. They were bound to have concerns about our 'rogue' group.

In 2006, I came to work for my current employer, the North Carolina Biotechnology Center (NCBiotech). I began as the library director with no IT responsibilities. In 2007, after meeting with directors and VPs about their issues and concerns, the new CEO heard a common theme: frustration with IT. A

---

1   Susan C. Speer and Daniel Angelucci. "Extending the Reach of the Thin Client," *Computers in Libraries* 21(2001): 46-50.

recent survey on satisfaction with IT support had shown satisfaction was low. In my first meeting with him, I talked about my background. He then asked: "Can you run an IT department?" I said yes! He checked that out and quickly promoted me to Vice President, Library and Information Services. Nearly ten years later, I am still managing the library and the IT staff.

Reflections

So, after 35 years as a librarian, working in and managing IT, I do have some thoughts about the role of librarians and women in IT.

The impetus for much of my early IT work was to find a better, faster, easier way to accomplish a goal or to solve a problem. Before we had an automated circulation system, our dilemma was that all of the books were due at the end of the semester and then we had a lot of overdue letters to send out. How can we do that as quickly as possible? Let's create a database in Dbase and write a program to print letters on our dot matrix printer!

This is just good innovation or problem–solving. It is not special to librarians, IT, or women. One reason the IT/library teams fit so nicely at NCBiotech is that the library had been the only group to claim ownership of a newly implemented client-relationship management (CRM) system. When I learned that a data steward would be hired to provide quality control in the system, I immediately knew the library should own that position. The position, filled by a librarian, soon grew into a CRM system administrator, working more with IT than the library. As the librarians began to use the system to manage a database of life science companies, we became experts in the system and other teams called on us to consult with them in its use. The lesson from this? Never define your job too narrowly. Take on new tasks no matter how removed they may seem from your role as a librarian.

One year while at Wake AHEC my boss gave me the highest score possible on my performance evaluation. He noted that he did that not because I was perfect, but because I set the right tone for the team. The customer service spirit that I constantly reinforced with the IT team made us successful. While I felt guilty about not being able to do as much hands-on IT as I had once done, he was telling me that the important part of my job was the customer service. As he said, the hospital IT team spelled service "C-O-N-T-R-O-L." I firmly believe that librarians carry that customer service gene with them wherever they go, including into IT.

In my experience, both women and librarians strive to prove their value and that is accomplished through service. Are women customer-oriented due to a maternal instinct? Are librarians customer-oriented to ensure survival? There have probably been studies on this. All I know is that this penchant for excellent customer service is critical to the success of libraries, but not to the success of IT departments. Especially in special library and hospital library settings, libraries can be seen as disposable. Only by providing excellent, innovative services do they survive. IT departments, on the other hand, are critical to every business. They provide access to mission-critical applications and they ensure data and network security. Not surprisingly, I have worked with male IT professionals who told me that IT should be in charge, dictating and controlling what staff can and cannot do. In my professional library experience, however, my colleagues are focused on solving the problem for clients, finding information they need, and using technology as a tool rather than an end in itself.

Just as I do not believe in using IT to control what customers do, I do not believe in micromanaging my staff. I hire the smartest person I can find – hopefully someone much smarter than me. I give them the parameters of operation and I let them work. My staff keeps me in the loop, runs things by me, and when needed, explains things to me – slowly, if necessary. It is more important to *know* what I am talking about than to pretend that I do. Good leaders – women, librarians, or otherwise –

have to put ego aside. I have learned that when I am open to hearing the ideas of others, a stronger solution than the one I imagined is the result.

I have also learned to let my ego go where salary is concerned. At Wake AHEC, I needed a good person to run our patient scheduling and billing system. That person's salary was more than I was making. The marketplace dictated the salary. When I was promoted to vice president at NCBiotech, I learned that the IT director suddenly working for me, made about $20,000 more than I did. It took a few years for my salary as a VP to catch up with his, even though I am certain he had the same – or fewer – years of experience than me.

Upon reflection, I don't believe that I have been discriminated against or viewed with a certain doubt about my skills because I am a woman. Sadly, I'm reminded of the response of my best male friend, when I told him I was going to graduate school for a master's in library science. He told me I was too smart for that. The IT person who complained I was just a f*ing librarian, didn't complain I was just a woman. A former IT employee here loved to complain that I knew library IT, not 'real' IT. (Is a server not a server, wherever it is deployed?). My librarian title is what has been disparaged.

Despite my gender or career, I have twice been given the opportunity – by male bosses – to show what I am capable of in terms of managing IT, and in both cases, I was successful. I'd like to think I'm helping to redefine "librarian."

In summary, I think we win when we do not define our jobs too narrowly and are open to broader contributions to our parent organizations. I think the rules of good management, leadership and customer service must always be applied to the jobs we undertake.

ESSENTIALISM, SOCIAL CONSTRUCTION, OR INDIVIDUAL DIFFERENCES

Jenelys Cox, Jeff Rynhart, Shea-Tinn Yeh

#Observations #Advice #ChangeAgents

Per the United States Department of Labor Women's Bureau's latest available statistics, the percentage of women employed in computer and information technology occupations was consistently lower than the average for all occupations. When broken down by selected characteristics, these numbers range from 12.4 percent in computer network architectures to 35.2 percent in web development.[2] Is this trend reflected in the libraries? Although no comprehensive statistics are available for women in library IT, Lamont's study does reflect the same trend in that the number of women as library IT department heads has been about one half that of men between 2004-2008.[3] Why is there an underrepre-

---

2   "Computer and Information Techology Occupations," *United States Department of Labor Women's Bureau*, last modified July 2015, https://www.dol.gov/wb/stats/Computer_information_technology_2014.htm

3   Melissa Lamont, "Gender, Technology, and Libraries," *Information Technology and Libraries* 28, no. 3 (2009). DOI: http://dx.doi.org/10.6017/ital.v28i3.3221

sentation of women in library IT leadership? Is gender a concern? To answer this question, a more essential question should be addressed, i.e. what makes a successful IT supervisor in libraries? We posit that a successful supervisor is reflected in the morale and self-esteem of their reports, as well as in the integrity, productivity, and efficiency of the department or group they head.

Based on our experiences, a supervisor may exhibit a broad spectrum of traits, from what is traditionally considered masculine to what is traditionally considered feminine. Our female supervisors are generally more understanding, compassionate, supportive, and likely to take a vested interest in their employees. They are also less likely to show aggression or anger. However, they may be seen by others as more easily manipulated and less commanding. In contrast, our male supervisors are generally more confident, commanding, and firm. They may be stronger leaders with higher expectations, but may also be more obtuse, aggressive, demanding, and unconcerned with the self-esteem or well-being of their employees.

We have found that a successful supervisor is aware of the importance of their subordinates' state of mind and can also exhibit firmness, organization, and confidence. It is therefore the combination of the more favorable personality traits associated with each gender that ensure productivity, reduce conflicts, and protect the morale of subordinates. These differences in traits have been highlighted in our work under male and female IT supervisors. Below are a few of our personal stories.

Story 1: I worked for a younger man who had very little supervisory experience. His self-confidence often prevented others from offering support or feedback which would have benefitted him as an inexperienced supervisor. He tended to respond to questions or requests for clarification from those under his supervision with aggressive or belittling phrases, such as "Why would you do that?" or "Of course. Think about it." Additionally, he balked at employee input on projects or workflows. The implications, whether perceived or factual, were that he considered his employees incapable of making decisions, lacking in value to the institution, and unworthy of his concern.

At another job, I worked for a small office and library with joint IT. Several short-term interns worked under a female head of IT who was a disorganized supervisor and often forgot which training or tasks had been completed and by whom. At one point, she had a week-long business trip to attend and only then realized she had not assigned anyone to maintain the website in her absence. Before her departure, she merely managed to give us a log-in without any additional documentation or instruction. Needless to say, we were left in a hopeless state during her absence.

In contrast, one of my more successful IT supervisors was a woman who was organized and managed to balance the needs of her employees and the work. She made her expectations clear and was firm about requirements. However, she also showed interest in her employees' lives and wellbeing. As a simple example, she found out that one of her employees had suffered an injury the previous night. She offered to allow them to go home to finish their work in comfort, since there was a project to which the employee could contribute from off-site. Her handling of the situation showed concern for the employee's well-being, demonstrated the value she placed on the employee's work, and reinforced her expectations that the day's work be completed.

Story 2: I was hired by a female supervisor holding a high-ranking position at the organization, overseeing other supervisors and employees. From the onset, the contrast between this supervisor and the male supervisor at my previous job was striking even though both supervisors are considered effective and skillful leaders. The female supervisor immediately established herself as a mentor, who would assist with any problems or difficulties I had, and offered guidance if I made a mistake. The male supervisor made it clear that he had a dominant personality type and hoped my personality type was not, or there would be conflict. This made him seem unapproachable, and created concern of his reaction to any mistakes I might make.

My work environment and personal experience was of concern to the female supervisor. She sensed my need for privacy, and enacted some changes to my work area to shield it from the view of others, without any request. This action immediately made me feel of value and that my work was considered important. Under the male supervisor, I was more likely to hide mistakes due to the uncertainty of his reaction, creating an unpleasant situation that often caused complications in the future. The female supervisor was always positive, giving me room to learn while affirming the nature of a mistake. She ensured that I was aware of the cause of the mistake, and discussed future actions to avoid repeating the situation. Overall, the mental and physical work environment established by the male supervisor was inferior compared to what was established by the female supervisor.

Based on these experiences, we have found that women who are good supervisors in library IT are compassionate and understanding, but also confident and decisive. They exhibit the most favorable traditional traits of both genders. On the other hand, our male supervisors are often confident and decisive, but are also uncaring, impatient, and aggressive. This discrepancy compounded with the statistics of male dominant IT leadership would suggest that today's supervisory positions maintain the emphasis of traditionally masculine traits. Naturally, women who do not possess masculine traits may avoid a position with a masculine expectation, whereas women who do possess masculine traits or are more willing to develop them may be drawn to the supervisory IT role. We conclude that this attraction or revulsion to a career IT leadership role is based on the individual's perception of the role and how much personal change is required or acceptable to attain it.

This brings us back to our initial query. If women can possess the qualities of a successful supervisor, why are they less likely to be IT supervisors? Trauth, Quesenberry and Morgan suggest that the reason is neither owing to "essentialism," which theorizes that women just are not suited for technological work, nor to "social construction," which theorizes that women can do the work but are hampered by social expectations. Instead they propose individuals respond to IT work in a range of individual ways.[4] We agree from our observations and analysis that the pursuit of a supervisory role in the IT landscape and success within that role can be attributed to individual preferences, experience, and personality rather than a sole factor of gender differences.

4   Eileen M. Trauth, Jeria L. Quesenberry, and Allison J. Morgan, "Understanding the Under Representation of Women in IT: Toward a Theory of Individual Differences," *Proceedings of the ACM SIGMIS Conference on Computer Personnel Research*. (Tucson, AZ, April 2004): 114-119.

WOMEN IN LIBRARY IT – ONE MAN'S PERSPECTIVE

Kevin Finkenbinder

#Observations #Advice #BreakingStereotypes #CareerPath
#Confidence #Perspective #TakeRisks

There is no doubt that IT is still a male dominated field. Even
within library IT departments, subjective evidence leads me to
believe that men outnumber women, but the difference is far
less in the library environment than in most of the technology industry. From my observation, it appears that there is still
a library IT gender gap, but it is much smaller than the gender gap in the nation at large. From my observations: female
under-representation in IT careers has identifiable (and repair-
able) causes, there are many reasons women are more represented in library IT than in the general IT community, and there
are ways female influence can expand in the IT community.

Underrepresentation of Women in IT Careers

My personal journey in IT started in about 1981 when I took
a computer programming class at a local University's summer
enrichment program for public school students. In this Pascal
programming class, the two instructors were female and 18 or

19 of the 35 participants were as well. From my early adolescent perspective, there was no discernable advantage or disadvantage to being male or female in the class. In fact, some of the female students I studied with seemed to sense the interaction of various programming constructs far better than the male students.

Ten years later, I transferred back to this same university as a computer science major. Only two of the dozen faculty members of the Computer Science department were women and neither of them was in a tenure track position. Of the thirty-five people in my Computer Science graduating class, five were women (about 14 percent). A similar percentage of new hires in my first several IT jobs were women – 10-15 percent, but the clear majority of the older IT personnel (more than 95 percent) were men.

In recent years, I have seen women make strides in representation of new hires (about one-third of the new hires are women) but the number of women I have seen hired is still far less than 50 percent. According to a 2014 Georgetown University study,[5] only 31 percent of students in computer and mathematics majors are female. Not all IT hires have a computer related degree, nor do all computer majors enter the IT fields, but if about one-third of the new hires are women and one-third of the computer science majors are women, the logical conclusion is that the barrier to women entering IT careers is at the education level, not at the hiring level.

To improve female representation in IT careers, the change needs to take place in the middle school and high school years. While admittedly anecdotal, my experiences show that early adolescent interest in IT is similar between boys and girls, so what changes between seventh grade and college admittance?

---

5   Anthony P. Carnevale, Jeff Strohl, and Michelle Melton, *What's it Worth?: The Economic Value of College Majors* (Washington, DC: Georgetown University Center on Education and the Workforce, November 2014), https://cew.georgetown.edu/wp-content/uploads/2014/11/whatsitworth-complete.pdf

From 2008-2013, I was a mentor for a high-school FIRST robotics team at Johannesburg-Lewiston High School in northern Michigan. We worked hard to get female students involved in the program but the "social clique" constantly stymied our efforts. When female students were approached about joining the group, a regular response was that the boys wouldn't like them if they were involved in something like that. We heard this response often enough that we surveyed boys in the school and found that only about 10 percent of those surveyed would be less interested in a girl in robotics. This 10 percent was apparently very influential on their female counterparts. Meanwhile 40 percent of the female students thought that a girl in robotics would be unattractive to most boys. Another common response was that their "BFFs" would disown them if they got involved in "dirty" technical activities. There was a final class of response when we asked a girl to join the robotics team. Although particular students may have had great grades in mathematics, drafting, computers, and other related classes, they would often respond that they did not know enough about robotics to be of any use; their male counterparts, with the same or worse credentials, would jump at the opportunity to stretch and expand into an area they wanted to learn.

The anecdotal evidence is that female teens had accepted social narratives that were holding them back in STEM (Science, Technology, Engineering, and Math) related educational/career choices. The surveys showed that, at least in this particular high school, these social narratives were, to a great degree, spread by other females. To improve female representation in IT and STEM careers, the social narrative of teens must improve.

Observations on Why Women Are More Represented in Library IT

If about one-third of IT related graduates are women, why are they better represented in Library IT? Of twenty-four IT related positions in my immediate area, twelve are held by women and the ratios of males to females are evenly split within authority levels and when evaluated by length of employment. What makes the library environment different from the general IT community? There are at least two major factors in the Michigan State University Libraries that have positively influenced this ratio...library hiring practices and library career tracks.

When interviewing for IT careers, "The most commonly reported method in the U.S. is one-on-one interviews (68 percent) followed by telephone interviews (56 percent), both of which have changed little since 2010."[6] In most of the IT world, a manager looks at the available candidates and then hires the best candidate. They may ask for input from others, but the available pool of candidates and the preferences of the hiring manager primarily influence the decision. The MSU Libraries' hiring practices are more communal. Here, committees are usually involved in the selection process for librarian and information technology staff positions. Most of these committees have representation from outside the position's area of expertise. While these committees are still advisory in nature, they create a broader cultural awareness in the process. Of necessity, the biggest focus of the hiring managers in both corporate and library environments is accomplishing the task, but individual prejudices may play an unrealized role in the selection process when two candidates are basically equivalent. The library committee hiring process brings much more attention to how the candidate will interact with the general library community. Since the MSU library community is less than 30 percent male, there is an awareness of the need to have women in all aspects of library life...including IT.

A second reason for the prominence of women in library IT is that there are many IT career tracks in the library that *do not*

---

6   Dr. Andrew Chamberlain, "Why Is Hiring Taking Longer? New Insights from Glassdoor Data," Glassdoor Economic Research, June 18, 2015,http://www.glassdoor.com/research/app/uploads/sites/2/2015/06/GD_Report_3.pdf.

begin with IT. Of the women in my library's IT related units, four came from a primarily IT background, the other eight have moved into IT related work from non-IT library backgrounds. These women are just as competent in their IT related tasks as those who came from a strict IT background, but found a different path to get here. It is my speculation that this alternative path into IT has allowed them to overcome the social bias that makes it more difficult for many women to enter STEM related college majors. Thus, while it is positive that the women have gotten into the library IT field, it is a stain on our society that the best path for them to do so is by way of an alternate career.

Ways to Expand Women's Influence in the IT Community

While the presence of women is growing in IT careers and specifically in library IT careers, there are areas where the influence of women can expand in the IT community. Like many libraries, we use the Drupal CMS in much of our web development, so I have been active in the Drupal community. According to the group Women in Drupal[7], 17 percent of the participants in the Drupal community are female, which is a huge improvement over the 1.5 percent in the general open source community. This same ratio of about 20 percent was present in the local Drupal conference that the MSU Libraries sponsored in the summer of 2016. However, only three of the fourteen self-nominated candidates for leadership of the international Drupal Association were women. Only one of the twelve self-proposed sessions for the local 2016 Drupal conference was submitted and presented by a woman.

I have worked with many women in IT. In many cases, their understanding and ability to present ideas about IT have

---

7   Jennifer Hodgdon (jhodgdon), Addison Berry (add1sun), Karyn Cassio (techgirlgeek), and Angie Byron (webchick), "Women in Drupal (Formerly DrupalChix)," *Drupal Groups*, September 25, 2014, accessed April 4, 2017, https://groups.drupal.org/women-drupal.

exceeded those of the general IT community, but for whatever reasons have chosen to exclude themselves from the places of influence in the community. Harvard Business Review referred to a statistic from a Hewlett Packard internal report: "Men apply for a job when they meet only 60 percent of the qualifications, but women apply only if they meet 100 percent of them."[8] This statistic may come from the realm of job application, but it also applies to job self-promotion. For whatever reason, men are willing to present themselves as an expert if they know a little more about something than someone else. Women tend to expect that if they are not *the* expert, then they cannot be viewed as *an* expert.

If women want to have their influence in the IT realm grow, they need to recognize that the pre-selection expectations of many people in the IT community are lower than many women place on themselves. *Please* put yourself out there. Volunteer to speak. Run for leadership positions. While ok_lyndsey, the screen name of a woman who ran for an open position on the Drupal Association board, was not ultimately elected, she lasted through ten of twelve rounds of voting, advancing far beyond most candidates.[9]

If women get more involved in these types of opportunities, there will be several positive effects. Women will have more influence on the attitudes of people in IT, making it less of a male run club. Women will have more influence on the hiring process as people look to leaders in the IT community for candidate recommendations. Most importantly, women will be positioned to help break the barriers that are keeping younger women and teens from seeing IT and STEM related careers as socially acceptable.

---

8   Tara Sophia Mohr, "Why Women Don't Apply for Jobs Unless They're 100% Qualified," *Harvard Business Review*, May 20, 2015, accessed April 4, 2017, https://hbr.org/2014/08/why-women-dont-apply-for-jobs-unless-theyre-100-qualified.

9   Megan Sanicki (megansanicki), "2017 Drupal Association at-large Election Winner Announced," *Drupal Association* (blog), March 27, 2017, https://www.drupal.org/association/blog/2017-drupal-association-at-large-election-winner-announced.

A Career in Library Technology: A Personal Essay

Julie Guzzetta

#Observations #Advice #CareerPath

I am a Library Technologist. Since 2007, I've worked with a small team supporting the public and staff technology in our library. Since there are so few of us, I've taken on a great number of roles over the years. I help deploy and maintain workstations, kiosks, some servers, peripherals, and other devices in the library, as well as provide user support for staff and students. In addition to these daily operations, our team has a running technology project list that we work on.

Prior to working in library IT, I was a systems analyst in a local government department, where I supported engineers and other business groups. I provided technology services to several department building sites, including two county airports. The system administration skills that I developed there provided a good starting point for working in library IT. When I started at the library, I was very eager to start familiarizing myself with library systems and operations. I was lucky to have supportive co-workers who could answer my questions, so that I could get started on the right track. There was so much to learn, it was difficult to know where to start.

I work with a small technology team, and I handle the bulk of support operations for our client/server environment. I'm the most visible member of the team, while the others remain behind the scenes. Since I'm very personable and approachable, people are comfortable asking me for technical help. These are personality traits that contribute to being successful in a support role. I also have a keen ability to gauge someone's level of technical understanding when conversing with them so that I can translate technical terms appropriately as needed. This unique combination of what are sometimes referred to as "soft skills," along with my technical expertise allows me to stand out from the pack.

One thing that is really rewarding about my job is that I get to know all of the staff in the library. One of my roles is to provide technology orientations to new staff and faculty. Most of the time I am the first technology team member to meet with new employees. I demonstrate how to navigate through their new computer environment, and show them all of the technology resources available to them. Also, since I help maintain staff computers and software setups, I often stop by to help troubleshoot issues. I enjoy getting to know my co-workers and learning about the work that they do in the library. This is also helpful for me because the more I know about how they are using technology in their jobs, the better I am able to provide effective support or make recommendations for new technology solutions. Some of the projects that I have worked on over the years have involved studying a specific workflow in one area of the library, and working with a manager or staff member in that area to test and implement new technology solutions.

I also enjoy working in public service. I help maintain the public kiosks, student loaner devices, classroom equipment, high-tech group study rooms, and our computer lab. I use different software tools to configure and maintain these computers so that students will have a consistent experience across devices. Sometimes I am called upon to help a student recover a file that they lost while working on a lab computer. In these instances, the student is often in great distress because they've lost a project that they've been working on for hours. It's always rewarding to be able to help them recover the document.

One of the first things that I noticed when starting this position, is that there are very few women working in IT positions on campus. There is a centralized IT structure on our campus, so most of the technology staff work in the central technology department. Our library team often collaborates with the central IT department in order to provide a consistent level of support for our staff and patrons. During the monthly technology campus meetings, I look around the room, and notice that there are very few women in attendance. In smaller project meetings, I am often the only woman present. For some reason, women aren't applying for these jobs. I've participated in hiring committees for a few technology job positions on campus and I've noticed a lack of gender diversity while reviewing the wave of applications for these jobs. As a woman in IT, I try to stay visible within the technology community on campus, and represent the interests of the library. This year I'm on the Technology Administrator Board, and I help plan the agenda for the monthly campus technology meetings.

My advice to women who are interested in becoming library IT professionals is to become familiar with as many technologies as possible. Look at a job posting for the type of job that you're interested in and research the various technologies that are listed as requirements. There are many free online tutorials that one can use to explore technology topics. Also, your local public library might have paid subscriptions to online education systems like Lynda.com. If possible, experiment with different operating systems and open source software on your computer at home. Check out the technology classes that your local community college offers. If you already have a library job, seek out the technology folks in your department and ask them questions. Read up on the latest technology trends and news on websites like Ars Technica[10] or Slashdot[11].

---

10   "Ars Technica," *WIRED Media Group*, https://arstechnica.com/.

11   "Slashdot," *SlashdotMedia*, https://slashdot.org/

Working as a technologist also motivates me to become a lifelong learner. As I read about new technologies and research different areas of the field, I discover that there is so much more that I want to learn. I'm currently taking some math and science classes and will possibly pursue another degree that might help expand my career path in different directions. I'd like to work towards some promotional opportunities in my career and become a manager or CIO of an organization.

BEYOND THE HORIZON – LEARNING NEW
SKILLS THROUGH THE INFLUENCE OF DIVERSE
COMPUTER PROFESSIONALS

Alisha Taylor

#Observations #LearnCode #Mentorship #Persist

Julie Guzzetta, also a contributor to this book, works as a Computer Applications / User Support Specialist at Portland State University Library. She has a visible presence and is one of the two women employed in a department of six. The other woman is a Content and Usability Strategist (and works part-time). Julie has informed me that she is frequently among just a handful of women attending meetings, conferences and other major IT events. I asked Julie, who is soft-spoken with a radiant smile, whether she finds this a difficult social and cultural dynamic, and she affirmed that it is a challenge at times. Nevertheless, Julie is quietly confident, holds her position well, and is respected by colleagues for her knowledge and her positive customer service attitude.

I met Julie when I joined the Cataloging & eAccess Department at Portland State University Library. My work involves searching for metadata in bibliographic records, a repetitive and laborious task. Searching for metadata was taking almost an hour per record. I approached a friend, a software developer (at Intel), and we collaborated over the course of several months to develop a product that automated the task. The app, HyperLC, provides another user interface layer on top of the Library of Congress Online Catalog website, to enable users to retrieve and download batch records for further data analysis. My input was to brainstorm the data flow diagram and design the user interface.

When the tool was developed, I demonstrated it to my manager, who requested that I present and install the product for my co-workers. I approached the IT department, and Julie readily performed the installations. After subjecting the product to group testing, we identified and fixed the bugs, and it was eventually time to roll out the upgraded software. This time, the IT department indicated that I should provide my colleagues with written instructions to perform the installation. I realized this was impractical given the level of knowledge of my co-workers. I started to learn Windows command prompts to find and uninstall the old version, and install the updated version in a shared folder on the network. I was able to do the installation for a couple of co-workers but soon reached the limit of my knowledge. Tentatively, I approached Julie and asked for help. Julie gladly taught me advanced Windows command prompts with instructions, and empowered me to perform the complete cleanup/installation. Julie's attitude and willingness to help was a complete breakthrough, and prevented the project from failing.

During the project development phase, I realized that I needed to learn to code if I hoped to move forward in my career as a professional librarian. On the advice of a colleague, I decided to learn Python, as it is a user-friendly scripting language for beginners. I asked Julie for guidance and she pointed me towards online tutorials, instructional resources, and local IT boot camps. However, my family expressed concern at this new turn in my career.

I initially sought advice from a family friend with a firmware background (embedded software in electronic devices).

He worked for five years in the field prior to getting a formal qualification (BS degree). Based on his experience, possibly of fighting his way upwards without a degree, I was advised that it would take me ten years to master programming. Technology and software evolve rapidly, and you need to keep pace. Due to tight project deadlines in the commercial high-tech world, a software product is released as soon as it is good enough, with low-priority bugs shelved for later resolution. In the early stages, there is not a lot of accurate information available on documented bugs. It takes hours of research, beyond regular working hours, to successfully adapt and implement new software tools. My family friend added that one needs a master's degree to get ahead in the computer industry.

I have an undergraduate degree in chemistry, with a master's in library science, rather than a background in computer science. Moreover, until this point, I had not invested late hours after work researching software developments. Both factors seemed to indicate that I did not have an aptitude for this type of work. My family friend advised that it would be better to collaborate with an experienced developer (if one is available). In effect, I was warned against wasting my time trying to achieve a difficult goal. Sometimes I struggle to bypass my South Asian conditioning in terms of gender-related behavior, in the sense that I place a high value on listening to family and cohesiveness. I gave a great deal of weight to the advice that I received in my family circle.

Discouraged, I turned to Julie for advice, who listened and helped me move past my doubts. I realized that my objective is to apply computer technology to the library science field (as opposed to research and development of commercial high-tech products). At this point, I could afford to build my knowledge of computer science whilst continuing to work, a class at a time, without investing in an expensive degree upfront. I returned determined to continue with online Python tutorials.

I plan to reach out to libraries who may adopt HyperLC. It is freeware and uses open-source binaries (Selenium Webdriver and Mozilla Geckodriver). The drawback of being limited to a niche is myopia – I initially failed to consider that decision-makers might not comprehend what the app does, let alone why it may be useful. My challenge is to identify appropriate venues and forums to promote the product. Julie has inspired me to move forward, and my confidence has grown.

More importantly, by her own example, Julie has shown me that soft-spoken women can hold a valuable role in the world of IT. I've realized how important it is to persist despite the initial doubts I experienced in my personal life. I started to spend my evenings and weekends programming. I found job descriptions for catalogers that mentioned a preference for scripting languages, and emailed those to my family. When I demonstrated my sincerity through my actions, and the need for some programming in my field, my family became supportive and was impressed when I wrote my first program.

A critical influence for a beginner is someone who is willing to offer guidance and support through obstacles, and in that respect, I am fortunate to have met Julie. I have discovered that if you are determined, and willing to learn, with a stellar attitude like Julie, there is a way forward.

#CareerPath

JUMP SHIP

Marcia L. Dority Baker

#CareerPath #Advice #BeBold #ChangeAgent #JumpShip
#Leadership

"You must be the change you wish to see in the world."
Mahatma Gandhi

I recently changed professions. Not the kind where you move up, or laterally in your organization, but the big "let's jump ship to another world" kind of move. I've done this before, back in 2001. I have a Master's degree in Museum Studies (instead of a teaching certificate much to my mother's chagrin!) but after working in a quiet historic house and museum, I wanted more activity. I attended the Museums and the Web 2000 conference where I was introduced to the impact that virtual technology has on history or the story of humans. The early 3D depictions of ancient cities were mind-blowing in scope and opportunity.

Apply for the Job You Want

With a new view of technology and my information gathering know-how, I applied for jobs at my local public library. While I received many rejection letters for jobs I was qualified for, ironically, I was offered the position I was most enthused for but had no experience in. This was my first instance of applying for the job you want (future planning) not the job that will bore you. I also realized that I should not disqualify myself from the unknown, but instead be open to options I did not know existed. I said "yes" to the job at my preferred branch library and a new career path that included a new building, new books, a lot of technology, and the opportunity to create and teach computer classes in a new computer lab with new computers – it was like Christmas!

Working at a branch library is similar to being a Jack-or-Jill-of-all-trades. While the bulk of my responsibilities were adult services, I spent time staffing the library service points, supervising volunteers of all ages, and assisting with summer reading. The library programming opportunities included in-house events such as sustainable architecture and landscaping, local food programs, and presentations by regional authors. These built relationships with community organizations by providing great resources to all library users. The common denominator in working at a branch library was the need for information–finding answers, applying for a job or learning to read. Each request was important to the customer and librarians did a great job connecting the best resources to the request. This was the early 2000s when the Internet, databases, and communication technologies were rapidly changing. Technology made it easier to share information, and frankly, was fun to learn and play with.

Stay Curious

After a few years of branch library scheduling and the desire to move up in the library world, I applied for a circulation supervisor job at the academic law library at the University of Nebraska. As a working mom, I needed to balance my professional life with family commitments. Instead of "doing it all," I made a decision early on to pick a few important things in my life and do them well. Once again, it was a job I was not really qualified for but was willing to learn. I knew I needed supervisory experience to be a good leader and was intrigued by what a law library was. My family schedule needed me home at night and on the weekends instead of being at the branch library. I said, "yes" to the job offer, spending several years working circulation by day and on my Master's degree in Information Science and Learning Technologies (MLS) by night and on weekends as life allowed. I quickly realized that while circulation was a critical library service, it was not the way I wanted to spend my career. My supervisor and the library director were very supportive of my continued education and excitement to try new things.

Say Yes to Opportunities Disguised as Requests

As I had library programming and technology experience, I said "yes" to many opportunities disguised as requests. The legal world was slow to adopt social technologies. This is the nature of the two worlds: one well established on tradition and rules, while the other is still the wild, wild, west of developing technologies. I saw the benefits of the law library having an online presence so I created and managed the library's Twitter feed, the Facebook page and a Wordpress blog. I also created presentations for library and law conferences and wrote "how-to" use social media articles for lawyers wanting to learn more about the web 2.0. I was interested in classroom technology and volunteered to respond to AV requests for help in the law school classrooms, courtroom, and auditorium. This opportunity showed me how faculty use (and break) technology in the classroom and how students engage with technology for learning. I also gained a vision of how technology will play an active part in the future of the legal profession and in higher education.

Develop Yourself, No One Else Will

When I finished my MLS, I was able to move into a tenure track librarian position at the law library. As I did not have a JD (Juris

Doctorate), I decided technology would become my specialty. As legal tech was a developing area, this allowed me to use my interest in technology and librarianship to become an expert in the field. The advice from my library colleagues was to take charge of and develop my career as nobody else has the same vested interest. This outlook gave me permission, so-to-speak, to seek out opportunities to collaborate with like-minded legal tech experts, build relationships outside of the law library, and take a chance on those requests that may not seem relevant in the present but paid off in dividends for my future self. As part of the tenure process, I wrote and published, researched and presented, and built a professional network of librarians, tech people and academic professionals. I recommend speaking up, asking to participate, and keeping an eye out for opportunities that are disguised as requests. To quote Thomas Edison: "Opportunity is missed by most people because it is dressed in overalls and looks like work."

Put Yourself Out There

Technology has enveloped our lives, and can blur the lines between our private and professional selves. Like it or not, this makes it easier to find information, help people outside of the work day and jump ship for a career change. While each of us needs to decide the correct balance of engagement in social networks, my experience is that social media opens doors to information and relationships that would have taken years to find and/or build. Yes, there are obnoxious people in the world, but don't let that stop you from being you. We need strong women in IT, on social media, in our libraries, and participating in our world. Life truly is an adventure, show up and make it better.

Some days I am not sure what I want to be when I grow up. This is my honest answer when my daughter wonders about her choice of a college major, asks me how to balance life and a profession, and questions the direction our world is headed. It is a tough job to explain "why" when I do not understand why. Instead I focus on making a positive impact in the arena where I live, work, and play. Rather than wonder what I should be, I've decided to do work that matters to me and provides the opportunity to make good changes and help people. Our future, a generation of daughters, is looking to us as leaders, change-makers, and positive workers who do not give up. Use technology to level the playing field, make career changes that work for you, and be kind to everyone you meet. That being said – be aware of the trolls, you are better than they are no matter how difficult they may be. Find your tribe for support, laughter and strength.

Jump, Life is Short

I enjoyed my work as a librarian and anticipate I will return to the field. I wasn't looking for a career change but attended an IT Leadership conference hosted by ITS (Information Technology Services) at the University of Nebraska-Lincoln (UNL). Two of the dynamic speakers shared their leadership journeys; how, as women in higher education technology they moved between careers and across campuses to lead their organizations as change makers. Their stories inspired me to make a change. Long-story short, I jumped ship from the law library to information technology. I applied for the job I was interested in, knew would challenge me, and was a good fit for the next chapter of my career. I am now an Assistant Director, Academic Technologies, leading the Learning and Emerging Technologies team that supports the learning spaces, the Learing Management System (LMS) and emerging tech opportunities on campus. I've built relationships with the Registrar's office, Facilities and Space Planning group, Office of Academic Affairs, Institutional Research and other colleges and departments to improve the learning opportunities across campus and online– anywhere faculty teach and students learn.

This phase of my professional career is only possible as my family commitments have changed once again. With my daughter going off to college, now is the time I can commit to being an involved leader on my campus. It's not that the opportunity was not available earlier – I have been at UNL for 13 years–but that I made the decision to be the best mom I could be first, then a librarian and now assistant director, second. Being a working mom has made me a better advocate on campus, team leader in my organization, and proponent for work-life balance.

Conclusion

I operate under the assumption I have another 25-30 years as a professional. I'm not sure what my future career path looks like and I'm okay with that. As a type-A person, I am organized, like a plan-of-action, and enjoy working. But, and that's a big but, I've learned that life is funny and I need to enjoy the moments I'm given. This includes staying curious, looking for new opportunities, both personally and professionally, and applying for a job that's outside your comfort zone – better to have tried than wonder what might have been.

My next goal was sparked by a leadership program I participated in and the big changes in our country this year (2017). I felt my energy and passion for educating our future generations could be harnessed by stepping up as a woman in IT. I want to be a CIO in academic information technology so that I can influence change in higher education. We need more women in IT, more women in higher education leadership roles, and to paraphrase Gandhi–more people willing to step out to be the change we wish to see in our communities.

THE STORY OF MY UNINTENDED JOURNEY INTO SYSTEMS LIBRARIANSHIP

Olufunmilayo Fati

#CareerPath #UnintendedLibrarianship

I applied for the position of a systems programmer with the Academic Planning Unit of the University of Jos. Months later, I was invited to interview for the position but with a different group of professionals who applied for the same position but with the university library. I thought I was being interviewed for the position of a systems programmer to work with the university's Academic Planning Unit. When I got my appointment letter months later, it stated that I had been appointed as a systems programmer to permanently serve at the university library. This was very surprising to me, so I went back to the university administration to thank and inform them that I did not apply to the university library's advertisement but to the Academic Planning Unit. However, they explained to me that this was the place the institution could offer me. I took it as divine and consequently reported to the university library as destined. Prior to this time, I never once considered working in a library or becoming a librarian.

I planned and was prepared to obtain my master's in computer science. This was my "first love," and why I work as a systems programmer for my library. However, my desire to pursue my master's of computer science was in a way crossed (though never too late) when I was "advised" to pursue my master's in library science. This advice did not really go down well with me. Nevertheless, I took the advice and went ahead and pursued my masters in library and information studies because I had no other option, not because I am a woman, but because as much as I wanted to pursue my interest in computing, I also had to satisfy the interest of my employer. I remember some of my mentors in the computing world, especially from my alma mater, did not hide their disappointment in me for going into librarianship. They openly expressed that computing is more lucrative, that I was one of the best in my class at school, and that I was doing well as an early career computer professional within the National Computer Association.

Even though I was initially against being in library school, I still put in my best effort. I found myself to be among the best in my class. Many of my colleagues believed I already had a deep understanding of librarianship, but I made them understand that I was just a programmer in a library and if they asked me, I would tell them that I had never wanted to be a librarian. I graduated as one of the very best in my class (something I did not realize then, because I was unhappy about not having my master's degree in computer science).

Shortly after graduating from library school, I began to meet professional colleagues (local and international) who made me understand the deep extent of my relevance and importance to librarianship. These colleagues believed in me, and did not hesitate to involve me in librarianship activities, locally and at international levels. They positively and greatly affected my career. I began to get involved in professional librarianship activities through participation, volunteering and learning. At last, I was able to discover that I am actually where I should be. I now realize that being a professional systems librarian is a plus. As a woman IT professional, my gender has not been a hindrance to my achievements in librarianship. In fact, I have found myself in situations where I was the only female selected for activities in areas generally presumed to be men's. Now I am a professional librarian and a professional computer scientist and this gladdens my heart.

As a systems librarian, I ensure rapid and appropriate response from the library to emerging trends in the theory and practice of information services, provide interactive online services including the library management system (LMS), and implement the library's strategic plan. I coordinate the library online registration, administer the university's institutional repository and facilitate effective management and use of library electronic resources. My duties also include monitoring of library networks and the installation, customization and management of all library software for online access. I provide training for all library staff in ICT (Information and Communication Technologies) related matters within and outside my library. I work hand-in-hand with ICT directorate staff to implement upgrades and new systems and to perform systems backups. I also participate in university library committees.

Today, I am fulfilled being a systems librarian. I love librarianship especially the area of systems librarianship. I am determined to contribute the best I can to the profession. I will–together with other colleagues who have the best interest of this profession in their heart–make librarianship an envy of other professions. Now I appreciate that "advice." Today, I can stand on the highest mountain to shout that I AM A SYSTEMS LIBRARIAN AND I AM VERY PROUD TO BE ONE. I deeply love my job as a systems librarian.

"I've Had the Perfect Job for Me": An Interview

Alexandra Gallin-Parisi and Donna Kaminski

#CareerPath #Biography #Interview

In February 2017, I sat down with Donna Kaminski at Trinity University's Elizabeth Huth Coates Library in San Antonio, Texas. Donna has an easy laugh, unwavering patience, a sly wit, and an unmistakable can-do attitude. Donna is that person who obviously knows more than you do, but who will never make you feel stupid.

When she started her first job at Trinity University in 1979, she worked part-time in circulation and part-time in the bindery, eventually moving to full-time employment in circulation, then in copy cataloging, and then to an authority control position. Briefly, in 1993, she enrolled in the Texas Game Warden Academy in Austin, Texas, temporarily leaving behind her library work, as well as her two young children, to follow her dream of becoming a game warden. As one of only four female cadets, she struggled with the constant harassment, denigration, and disregard from male peers and supervisors. She ended up quitting the Academy after she sustained injuries that were consistently ignored by training personnel.

Without a college degree, she was nervous about finding another job she would enjoy. Fortunately, she was able to return to Trinity; eventually, she resumed her old authority control position, and then, in 1996, began her current position. Her workdays in the mid-1990s involved arriving at 7am to put commands into the mainframe computer, running appropriate reports, walking over to the Computer Center to chat with the people in IT, picking up reports, printing and filing card catalog cards, and using FrontPage to maintain the library's website. In 1999, Donna was the person who not only physically set up 87 individual computers for staff and students, but also played a pivotal role in training staff on using a computer mouse and Pine (email). She also created circulation rules in the ILS, ran data cables, set up printers, and performed all other technology-related tasks.

Her title changed in 2002 to its current form—Technical Support Coordinator—and she remained busy, helping get staff trained on the Microsoft Office Suite, troubleshooting the website and online databases, and managing hardware in the library. Over the past 15 years, her job has evolved to the point that it is not quite recognizable as the same work. While for some library staff, she is still the person to call when you need assistance with equipment, most of those issues are handled by the University's ITS Department through an online ticketing system. If staff members have a problem with software, they will more likely do web searches on their own to solve the issue. Today, Donna supports interlibrary loan, sometimes works on the website, and does other odds and ends around the library. I asked her to share some of her story with us. Too often, I feel that early-career women forget to listen carefully to the experiences of the women who have come before us. Below are excerpts from our hour-long conversation.

AGP: Were there other women working with you on technology in the library back in the earlier days?

DK: Yes. And that's actually kind of an interesting story. Ruby Miller, who was the Associate Director of Technical Services or something like that, was my supervisor, and she was and is an amazing woman. She's really probably the one you should interview! She just kind of had this affinity for computers. And she worked with a group of people and they developed MARCIVE. Have you heard of MARCIVE? Well, they moved off and had the company MARCIVE, but first, we were like their first customer. And so they did our authority control in an automated way, and they printed our catalog cards for the card catalog. And I actually had someone who assisted me in setting things up for everyone during that fun time of setting everyone up on computers. There was a librarian, Clare Dunkle, who was very...? I don't know exactly? You know how you just have some people who have no background in computers but who just kinda get it? So Clare and Ruby and I were kind of a team. And so at that time, Clare and I were actually building the computers. We would start with a brand new computer out of the box and we would just start installing stuff. And we had to install the operating system, and all that.

AGP: But how did you know how to do that if neither of you had any background?

DK: Well, we just worked really well together and we worked really well with the IT people. So they would show us once, and then they would just let us go. And we took notes, and if we had questions, they were our resource. But we just figured it out most of the time on our own.

AGP: So you, Clare, and Ruby are all women… Were there other women in ITS?

DK: Yes, so we were all women working in the library, with ITS in what was then called the Computer Center, who were all men. They kind of treated the library specially, since we had so much of our own software, and, honestly, we were just very competent. So they would show us what to do and just let us go. And it also took a load off of them because they were in the same position as we were, also getting computers out to everyone, needing to learn all about networking and all that stuff. So it was very, very busy. I was fortunate that Ruby had created such strong working relationships with the men in the Computer Center, and she encouraged me to do the same and have strong personal connections to the guys there. And so, no, I'm not a computer geek, but I could understand what they were telling me. And it was important that I could then translate what they were telling me into library language. They would say something and I wasn't afraid to ask, 'well, what does that mean?' and I became more of a liaison between IT and the library. So if we needed something from them, I could translate the library part for them because I had the experience in circulation and technical services and I knew the MARC tags which they didn't know. It was definitely all men in the Computer Center and the three of us women working with them on the library's technology side.

AGP: Do you feel now that your job is obsolete?

DK: I feel like when I leave here that, first of all, I think I will take a lot of knowledge with me that I've gathered over the 35 plus years I've been here. And that would be ok I think. I think the library will get along just fine. They'll just develop new ways of doing things. Like some of what I do will go to someone in Circulation, a lot of what I do with the ILS and Illiad, that will all go to other people, I have the feeling that my job will be kind of just pieced out.

AGP: How does that make you feel?

DK: A few years ago, it was a really difficult thing for me to grapple with. I was feeling like most of my job was being taken away from me. But you know, I am getting closer to retirement, in four or five years from now, and I think it's just the evolutionary thing to happen with this kind of job. Why should I hold things close to me that someone else can learn to do? So part of me was very protective. It's like, if you take everything away from me, what am I going to do? But then I just had to come to terms with the fact that I'm still needed, and that I'm still useful, just not in the same ways I was before. And that there are people who are just as capable.

AGP: How did you come to that resolution of your feelings?

DK: It was a process. It was just a process. You know there were days that I just didn't even want to be here. I guess I've always been the type of person that… like when I was younger, I could be very reactive, but over time I've learned that I can just sit and wait things out, and it'll all fall into place. I've been here 37 years and over that time, there's been a lot of change, and I had to decide to either not like the change enough to leave or to want to stay and adapt. And so over all that time, I've just been adapting. And you know, it's not one of these things that one night I go to bed upset and the next morning I wake up and think, "Oh it's fine now." It's a process of coming in and dealing with, you know, touchy issues with people, and just kinda working until it falls into place, and then it's ok again.

AGP: Well, that sounds very hard. I know I'm more of a reactive type person.

DK: I've never felt possessive at work. It's just my job. So when people would get all hot and bothered about the colors on the website, I'm like, just decide and tell me and I'll do it. And so part of that I think is what's helped me to evolve personally with my job, where I'm not super attached to one thing and want to hold on to it, like "that's my website" "that's my ILS." It's like this is just my job and if you tell me what you want me to do, I'll do it the best way I know how to.

So I used to be the source person. The help desk people wouldn't even talk to you unless you'd talked to me first. And so somebody would maybe email them or call them and they would call me right away and say, "Hey, someone called us. What's up with so-and-so, have you looked at their computer?" And I'd say, "No but I'll go look and see." And most of the time it would be something I could fix. And the few times it wasn't, I would let them [ITS] know and I would be the one who would know how to word it so that they would really know what needed to be done. But over the last few years, it's kind of developed into a new thing. Like they're using a tracking system, so if I report something through that tracking system for you, then you don't see what's happening with that ticket. So I like to do the troubleshooting, and I'll help you word it if you need that, but it really makes more sense for you to submit the ticket yourself so that they can contact you and work with you to get your problem fixed.

AGP: Does that make you feel sad?

DK: A little bit. I see that there's less of a need for some-one to intervene. Because really, my grandkids, when they graduate from high school, they're probably go-ing to know how to program, and I'll tell you, I'm not a programmer. I could learn it fine, but do I want to learn it at this point in my life? Not necessarily. So the new people coming in here, they've got all this knowl-edge that maybe at one time was very difficult to come by. You needed a person there or you needed a book. There would be a lot of times someone would ask me how do you do this in Excel. I would say, "I don't know but I can figure it out." And in a way, it was just me knowing how to look it up. Because maybe they tried to look it up and didn't find anything or they found something and didn't know what it meant. So I think I served a really useful purpose. For a time. But now with you youngsters coming in [laughter], well y'all are very knowledgeable and not afraid of com-puters and not afraid of breaking anything and you're just gonna try stuff. Well, like you're using a Mac right here, and I don't use a Mac, so how helpful can I really be to you? Probably not at all.

AGP: Do you have any tips or advice or things women in academic libraries should know about working with mostly men doing IT stuff?

DK: I think academic libraries are different than if you're going out and working IT in a business. Because it is more of a community [in universities], and so it's not as cut-throat. But you just have to kind of take the time to earn their respect, and not just demand it, without them really knowing you. You definitely have to take the time to earn that respect because it isn't just going to be there. They aren't just going to automatically give you respect.

AGP: Do you feel that way especially as a woman working with IT men, or just any person working with an IT team?

DK: I guess it would be for any person working with IT. But, yeah, I do think especially as a woman. And I guess a strong feminist would, you know, protest against that, [laughter] but that worked for me. And that was what I learned from experience. And I work with a bunch of people, the people over there [in ITS], the ones I know and respect and the ones who know and respect me, we're not afraid to forget a term or to say "You know, I don't know about that, I haven't heard about that," and to just kind of bounce things off each other. Even the men will do that with me now, now that they know me and trust my judgment. It's just not that competitive as far as I'm concerned. I'm not competing with them in any way. Now if the library were to hire somebody new to be an IT person for the library now, like, another woman, then that's probably gonna change, and my approach might not work anymore. [...] You know, I've never really cared that someone thinks I'm super smart. I feel like I can learn something and share it with other people. That's my favorite part of my job, having an excuse to talk with everyone in the library and work with everyone. I feel so privileged to be here when I was here, at such an exciting time, a really fun, exciting time, with all the changes in computers and everything, and getting to learn new things, and to see what it has evolved to be. I've had the perfect job for me. And I was never going to try to compete with the men because I just wasn't afraid to say when I didn't know something or how something worked. That just worked out well for me.

AGP: Any other advice for women in library IT?

DK: Speaking just for me, I have found that men in IT tend to be more competitive, and less sharing. So they are responsible for one thing or two things or three things and I've seen where they hold on to that because that's theirs and they don't want to let anyone else touch it. Or they kind of worked out their little hierarchy between themselves and they know how things work for them within their group. And so if you come in trying to impress them, or compete with them, I think you put yourself at a disadvantage. My approach was just to do my research, know the terminology, go to them and admit when I didn't know something and not be afraid to show them that I understood what they were saying. And so you can't just be, "oh, whatever you say," but you can't just go in there and say "things need to be done my way." I guess, I mean, well I don't know if this is stereotyping or too sexist or anything, but it seems like, to me, men still have a problem, in general, taking that aggressive approach from women in the workplace. So I think with that fine line between assertive and aggressive, I would go more assertive. I'm not afraid to say, "Hey, you're the expert on this, and tell me what I need to know." So if you're wanting to be the expert, or rather, if you are the expert, don't hide it. But if you're not, don't be afraid to say you're not.

My Journey Through Library IT

Robin Hastings

#CareerPath #Advice #BeConfident #StretchGoals

Technically, it all began with the free web space (two whole MegaBytes!) that came with a dial-up account with AOL. That got me tinkering, and then exploring, and then venturing out into the wider world of HTML and Internet websites. I had accounts with Geocities and Angelfire (it's a wonder I don't put a spinning envelope gif next to each email address I encode into a website to this day). I played and learned as I went along.

One day, while in the local mall, I ran across a guy I'd once worked with at Waldenbooks. He was walking around with his best friend, the Computer Services supervisor for the local public library. Talk eventually worked around to the fact that they were looking for an assistant to the Computer Services supervisor who could both wrangle HTML and create a database in Access. I had those skills. I applied. I began working in the IT department (before it was called that) the last week of December, 1998.

In May of 1999, we moved the six public computers that were available near the reference desk to the basement, tripled their numbers and opened the Public Computer Center. I was put in charge of that, in effect, if not in actual job title (at least for a while–I did eventually carry the title of PCC Coordinator, but that was a bit later on). I did monthly computer classes, trained staff, and tinkered with technology in between. The original Computer Services supervisor moved on and a new IT manager was hired. I hadn't even considered applying for the job myself–I didn't think I was qualified and so I self-selected myself out of the job completely. The guy who was hired for the job was a Windows guy, but he didn't begrudge my working on the Linux server in the server room, so we got along fine.

I was sporadically attending college during this time–but I was also solo parenting a young man (he was little more than a toddler when I first started at the library) and so attendance was in fits and starts. I did find a 100% online program through the University of Phoenix at a time when no one else was offering that kind of thing and transferred my credits there to try to finish up a degree in information technology. When that "new" IT manager moved on to his next job, I felt more qualified to lead a tech department, so I applied and got the job. I was able to step into that role with the understanding that I'd have my degree within 4 years. It took 2 ½ years, so I made it in plenty of time.

While serving as the IT manager of the local public library, I don't remember having too many issues related to the fact that I am a female. I did have a memorable incident when a middle-aged man came up to me at the PCC desk and asked to "talk to your IT guy." I informed him he was. The look on his face has stayed with me to this day–sort of both incredulous and irritated is how I'd describe it. I don't remember his question, but I do remember he asked it, I answered it and he left satisfied. I dealt with the constant assumptions (not always by men–many women also made assumptions) that whatever man was behind the counter was in charge, even after I became the IT manager at the library. I also ran into the occasional vendor who, metaphorically at least, patted me on the head and told me not to worry my pretty little head about the details. The implication that I couldn't understand the technological under-pinnings of the software or service he (and it was always a he) was selling was clear. Sometimes it was subtle–just a reluctance to answer specific questions about the software and a redirection of my questions to less "tech-y" topics. Other times it was a more blatant statement that the technology behind the software or service was difficult and I wouldn't likely understand it. I made sure to use other vendors in those cases.

Eventually, after 14 years at that library, I read a job announcement, via the PUB-LIB listserv, advertising a position as the Director of Technology Services at the Northeast Kansas Library System (NEKLS) in Lawrence, KS. Glancing through the job duties, I felt I could do the job, but then I saw one of the requirements–an MLS. I sent an email to the director of the system, asking if that MLS was a "hard" requirement, since I felt that with 14 years of experience working with libraries and information technology, I could do the job. By this time, I'd also written a book or two. I had also written several magazine articles–the first of which was suggested by my director at the public library at which I worked at the time following a successful "24 Things" style program I'd helped lead–and presented at conferences around the world. So my name was "out there" as they say. He responded fairly quickly with the news that, yes, the MLS was a hard requirement, but they were very interested in my candidacy, so they would re-run the job and make it a "soft" preference in the next search–I was invited to apply at that time.

Moving to Lawrence, KS after having lived all my life in Jefferson City, MO was a change. As I struck out on my new adventure, I left behind my parents, my long-term boyfriend and my son. (He was just a few months into his senior year of high school, active in the band, and had no desire to move. So, he stayed with my parents while I moved three hours away for my new job. The director of the system assured me that I did not have to get my MLS to keep the job, but if I decided to do that, they would be very generous in helping me. Generous turned out to include 100% of the tuition costs, I just had to pay for my own books. Their generosity was and still is greatly appreciated. I also received and appreciated the apology my mother gave me for constantly yelling at me to get off that stupid computer and do something useful in the AOL era.

I took the full two years, but I did end up getting my MLS and, at that point, a job title change. I now serve the NEKLS organization as the Library Services Consultant–though my focus on services still tends to the technological, just because eighteen years of experience in that is hard to ignore. That job change happened just six months ago (as of the time of writing of this essay) and I'm still feeling my way into what kind of library services I'll be supporting. My coworkers, staff, and the librarians with whom I work have been almost universally accepting of my femaleness in this position and I have yet to encounter a vendor in this job that, even metaphorically, pats my head and dismisses me as a mere girl.

I'm not sure what lessons you might be able to tease out of my experiences in library IT from this recounting. I have butted up against sexism, though less so than others I realize. I have had to go outside my comfort zone to assure someone that I am capable of doing a job despite not having the required credentials (something I encourage all women to do–don't assume that the requirements for any job are always "hard" requirements!). I have been lucky enough to be able to be active in the library profession as both an IT person and, lately, as a librarian – both of my employers have supported my service to the profession. Reading stories of IT professionals in other fields makes me fully aware that I have had to overcome far fewer obstacles in my professional life than some, but they have popped up occasionally and they have been infuriating when they do. It helps, though, to be in a position to deny those dismissive men, who work for some vendors, my library's business in return. Being in a female-dominated profession as a practitioner within a male-dominated industry has smoothed my way considerably, I'm sure, but more work has to be done to encourage more women (and minorities!) to take a chance, stretch their wings and overcome their own personal obstacles in order to contribute their skills and talents to the world of library IT.

Not the "Same As It Ever Was": An Accidental Systems Librarian

Amy Hezel

#CareerPath #Accidents #Future

"… And you may ask yourself / Am I right? … Am I wrong? / And you may say to yourself / My God! … What have I done?!"–
Talking Heads, Once In a Lifetime

This song often comes into my head when I am asked: "How did you become a systems librarian?" I look behind me, sure the question is aimed at someone else, and then with the shock of realizing the question is for me, I say to myself: "My God!… What have I done?!"

When I applied to library school in 2000 and started the program in 2001, it seemed rather nifty and practical; I was taking a step in the right direction towards adulthood and it aligned with my current job. I was working as a researcher and library assistant at an art museum library. I was assisting curators with research on upcoming exhibitions and was helping with just about anything that came up in the library–working with students and community members on research questions, checking in serials, organizing the fascinating ephemera collection of artists' files, and eventually participating in the transition from card catalog to online catalog and using an integrated library system (ILS).

Fast forward several years. I had crossed the country – moving from Buffalo, to Des Moines, to Iowa City, to Oakland – and along the way had worked in a number of different libraries including an earthquake library, a digital archive, an academic library, and a public library. I was a new transplant to the San Francisco Bay Area, jobless and pregnant: "And you may ask yourself / Well … How did I get here?" Yes, I did ask myself this. More practically, I needed to find a job and as with past moves, I saw the switch to a new geographical location as an opportunity to make a change in my career and in doing so, discover something new. Thus far, my experiences in libraries were varied. "What was next here in the Bay Area?", I wondered. I applied for library jobs, though given the associated increase in cost of living with my new locale, along with the impending reality that I would soon be supporting another being, I was not particularly targeted in my search and was keeping an eye out for anything that just might work (fingers crossed!). I spotted a job posting that seemed so unthinkable that I had to apply out of pure curiosity, even if I was scoffed at for thinking I had any business applying. The posting that caught my eye was for a systems librarian with an ILS vendor. I remembered the days at the art museum when we transitioned to and began using a real-deal ILS. This transition was fascinating to me (though my role was peripheral). Maybe this would be an opportunity to learn more about these transitions, to learn more about how ILSs are constructed, and by gosh, to learn what in the world it means to be a systems librarian.

The reason I had no business applying for the job was because at that point I had very little experience working with library systems as a whole and even less knowledge – in fact zero, zip – in computer science or software engineering. This may be fairly typical of my generation of library school graduates. It seemed so many of us were in library school because of our backgrounds in liberal studies. We shied away from science and math, and embraced literature and art. Yet, library school is deeply technical. Learning the details of AACR2 or breaking down a MARC leader by byte is more similar than we might realize (or allow ourselves to realize) to breaking down a PERL script or Postgres query.

I think women in librarianship don't always make this connection and therefore remain intimidated by the systems and information technology side of things. On the other hand, some of us at very small libraries or with very limited resources (and maybe too often that is too many of us) are forced into situations where we have no choice but to try and wrestle with technology we previously found intimidating or unknowable. I certainly didn't make the connection between the skills I had learned in library school and the skills needed to work with systems and software when applying for the position. Rather, I came to know this through the experience of trying to learn and being given the opportunity to do so.

So yes, lucky for me, I got the job and over the course of the next nearly ten years, I learned skills and became interested in topics previously unfathomable to me. I learned fundamentals like Unix and delved deep into Apache and Lucene. I also learned the very real panic that arises from librarians when software breaks. What will they tell their staff, but more urgently, more importantly their patrons? I gained a strong understanding of ILSs and how the various components work (or don't work) together as a system. I learned all this thanks to amazing colleagues and a tremendous manager. Collectively, they generously shared their skills with me, while also granting me room for making mistakes and showing patience along the way.

Yet, all the while my heart pined for the past ... not necessarily for a particular place or job, but for a stronger connection with libraries and librarians. My decision to become a librarian was rooted in the experience of working in an art museum library, but that wasn't what I longed for particularly. Rather, it was the experience of being in a library and connecting information-seeking people with resources. My time in academic and public libraries reinforced this. For me, there was something unequivocally satisfying in being able to connect people lacking information with the materials they needed. It seemed then working for an ILS vendor there was something haunting me; there was something missing that had once been present. It became apparent that I needed to find a way back to a library. I needed the direct connection with the library and the people using the library. The question remained: How could I put my technical skills to use and bring those skills back to a library?

I found the way to use my skills in a library by working with their ILS. In this role, I feel I am able to participate more directly in the act of connecting people with information. Thus far, I have found a way to bring the technical skills I acquired as a systems librarian outside of the library, into the library. The knowledge I gained informs the answers I am able to provide regarding the ILS and I am more readily equipped to troubleshoot ILS related problems. Significantly, I am also able to connect students, faculty, and community members with the information they need whether at the reference desk, through an instruction class, or by way of troubleshooting an access issue.

My time as a librarian has certainly not been the "same as it ever was." And, I am grateful for this and my unexpected path to systems librarianship (even if it was accidental). But, had you asked me as a fresh faced library school student, dewy-eyed at the idea of Dewey: "Would you consider a career in Library IT or systems librarianship?" I would have said: "No way, I won't and besides, I can't!" But now? Now, I can say I am interested and capable (though always needing to learn more). Still, I may say to myself: "… Am I right? … Am I wrong?… My God! … What have I done?!" and likewise: "Do I really belong here?" What does it mean to be a woman belonging to the field of systems librarianship? Through the mere act of questioning: "Do I belong?" I am doubting I belong.

Yet, I hope I'm wrong. I hope the current and new generations of library school graduates are open and hip to the connections between computer science, software engineering, and library school, even if their backgrounds are not in these areas. I hope my female colleagues new to the field are seeking jobs that overlap in all of these areas. We know women are a dominant part of the library workforce. We also know that proportionally there are not enough women in those upper management and leadership positions. Therefore, I'd love to see the new generation of women in systems librarianship and those working in library-related IT advocate for their roles at the top. That vantage point is unique in that it contributes to the kind of knowledge – both the breadth and depth – that can fuel a leader for the future without having to look back and without having to ask: "Do I belong here?"

Library IT is Never Boring

Tari Keller

#CareerPath #Advice #ExcitingCareer #History

What can you do with an arts and sciences mathematics degree, when you know you do not want to go to graduate school for mathematics? You teach. I taught junior high math for five years, while working on a master's degree in educational media. Math labs were a big thing then.

To do anything with my master's degree I needed a masters in library science. I went to Indiana University (IU) Library School. My first course, in current library issues, required writing three simple programs in a string language. I worked with two other women on the programs. We had so much fun working together that we took a class in creating databases. The students in the database course were mostly men. Most of the students in the IU program took the searching databases course. I also took two cataloging classes.

When I took my practicum at the local high school, the high school librarian wanted to know why a math major would want to be a librarian. My liberal arts background meant nothing to her. I decided to go into academic librarianship. I was fascinated with the Machine-Readable Cataloging MARC format and its structure. What was happening in my home state of Ohio with Ohio College Library Center – now Online Computer Library Center (OCLC) was exciting. My first job as a librarian was as general cataloger at the University of Kentucky (UK). I was hired for my Bachelor of Arts degree in Mathematics. I cataloged engineering and mathematics monographs and theses mostly.

After five years of cataloging, I became the Head of the SOLINET (Southeastern Library Network) Quick Cataloging Unit, which edited and ordered UK's cataloging cards from OCLC. While I was in charge of the unit, we moved from terminals to using dual floppy microcomputers. We were beta testers for the OCLC Cataloging Micro enhancer, which allowed us to batch upload our cataloging records after entering or editing offline.

In 1983, Michael Lach, Associate Director for Public Services, along with a small committee, investigated automating the circulation operations of the library system. Around that time, OCLC bought a medical library system and started developing it for other library types. They called it LS/2000. Our Director, Paul Willis, along with Mike, decided we should go with a system that could provide a public catalog, along with cataloging and circulation functionality. I talked my way onto the planning committee with "How can you do this without having someone who knows the record structure that is the foundation of the database?" Given my experiences and knowledge, plus the contributions I made to the LS/2000 planning project, Paul and Mike asked if I would like to be the systems librarian for UK.

We went live on OCLC's LS/2000 in 1984 with our Data General server running in the university's Computing Center. I learned to make RS-232 serial cables by sitting on the floor of the machine room with a young man who would eventually become one of the university's networking gurus. He taught me to troubleshoot our network interface units. During this time,

I also upgraded our dual floppy microcomputers by installing hard drives and more memory.

Working closely with the Computing Center administration and staff, we selected our initial staff and public terminals. Working with the campus Physical Plant Division, we installed networking connections to all eleven libraries in the system. I worked with library committees to plan the configuration of the software. Although we had the Computing Center doing our nightly tape backups, I learned how to run the server console, do the backups and power down the computer. Initially there were three librarians rotating responsibility for the pager. The associate director's wife got tired of the beeper going off in the middle of the night for a problem with the server. Our head of Circulation liked to use it when her children were with a babysitter, but the late-night calls were a problem for her family. Being single and the lowest administrative rank, I carried the pager the most. I had it the night there was a fire in the machine room. I had to go in to power down the Data General, since the operators all were dealing with the mainframe and peripheral systems.

I did have trouble with one of the operators who did the library systems backups. He had problems taking orders from a woman. After a number of complaints from a female operator and me, he was let go. I also had trouble with repairmen from another computer company, when they put their tools and manuals on my computer. They leaned against one of the disk drives and accidentally turned it off causing the LS/2000 to go down. I gave them a hard time for being so clumsy.

In 1989, it was time to find another system. We had pushed the limits of what the LS/2000 could do. Campus information technology and the university president said we had to run the next system on the MVS (Multiple Virtual Storage) part of the campus IBM mainframe. After looking at systems that promised they would run on the IBM soon, we went with NOTIS, a system developed by Northwestern University and used by many academic libraries. Campus IT hired a systems programmer for the library system to handle the Basic Assembly Language programming and technical details of our using the mainframe. I really could not do that job and my job too. I was involved in the interviewing process. Dave Block came from a utility company, but quickly learned the ins and outs of library work. Initially we had a female program analyst from campus IT assigned to our project. She did not understand our priorities and it was like playing a game of "telephone" with her in the middle directing our programmer's work. She moved on to another project. Dave listened to all our needs and working closely with him, we were able to automate the loading of patron records, paying vendors, and all our nightly jobs.

I worked with Jack Coffman, the campus IT security officer, to set up our MVS user accounts and ran the library's part of the disaster preparedness drill annually. Jack also attended IU as an undergraduate, so we had something in common to talk about. I served on the campus Y2K Preparedness Committee and provided documentation on all our library systems and equipment to assure we could still work on 1/1/2000. This was a group of middle managers from across campus who were responsible for overseeing their units systems and desktop computing.

Dave Block also helped with our implementation of OCLC's WebZ SiteSearch to provide a browser-based OPAC for our NOTIS database, and the Multiple Database Access System databases we had. That led to Dave's and my involvement in 1997 with the Kentucky Virtual Library, our multitype library consortium (KYVL) implementation of WebZ for Kentucky's shared commercial databases and library catalogs. The University of Louisville negotiated a contract with Endeavor to buy Voyager and included wording to have it possible for the rest of the state universities and colleges to purchase the system under their contract. In 1999, KYVL received money to buy Voyager for the rest of the Kentucky state institutions. The University of Louisville was considered phase one. Five other state institutions were in Y2K trouble, so they implemented Voyager in 1998-99 as phase two, as it was designed to work on day one of 2000. The remaining three institutions, including UK, already had migrated to the Y2K certified releases of their current systems, so they would be in phase three. The Chairman of the KYVL Technology Committee took a sabbatical in 1999 and he suggested I become the committee's chairperson, since I was coordinating the KYVL WebZ project for the committee. The KYVL Advisory Council agreed. For the next seventeen years, I led the KYVL Technology Committee as it morphed into the KYVL Voyager Consortium. This is somewhat ironic, since UK was in the third phase of the Voyager project, and implemented the system in June 2000. There were many meetings with campus IT leaders about how to equip the statewide consortium. I was involved in these mostly male meetings. Throughout the seventeen years of the KYVL Voyager consortium, I coordinated working with our server administrators on both campuses, Endeavor, and eventually Ex Libris. We upgraded the servers once and then moved the databases to the cloud with Ex Libris. The consortium grew from nine state-supported members, to include two state government libraries, six private universities and two corporate libraries. We worked toward consensus with our decisions. We relied on conference calls and doodle polls to make it all work.

When we were looking at the next generation of integrated systems, we made a report and recommendation to KYVL and to the State-Assisted Academic Library Council of Kentucky (the state university deans). It was clear that we would not get much, if any, KYVL funding for this move. State funding was scarce. The private universities and government libraries were exploring OCLC's World Share system. Some of the state-supported universities' library deans felt they could do better on one system and some another. Each made his or her own decision. Four of the state universities, including UK, negotiated with our Voyager vendor and migrated to Alma and Primo in 2016.

In the beginning, I was the only one working with the system, hardware and software. I had one student to assist me. I earned my reputation with campus IT in the 1980s and built on it with every new system. I went into each new situation confident, having done my homework, asking questions when I needed information or help with a problem, and showing no fear. I made a few presentations in my early years at the annual Kentucky Higher Education Computing and Communications Conference, which impressed the men, and I showed interest in their work as well. I treated everyone with respect and received respect in return. It did not hurt to be in a campus culture where women always have had a place in information technology, like UK. Now I am in the Library Information Technology Department. My supervisor, who is a librarian, and the four other staff in the department are men. We have two desktop support staff, one network and systems administrator and one programmer. I handle the integrated library system back office and discovery system while they do the other technical work. They help me with programming when I need it. They handle the API work, as I am working on configuring the two systems. It does not seem to be a big deal to them that I am a woman.

IT AND LIBRARIES: A PERFECT CAREER MARRIAGE

Karen Knox

#CareerPath #KnowYourStrengths #LibraryLeadership
#TechnologyAdvocate #TechnologyInLibraries

When I first went to college for undergrad at the University of Michigan, I decided I wanted to study computer science (CS). So I got a bachelor of science in CS and went off to work as a programmer at IBM in Austin, Texas, never having given libraries a passing thought. I enjoyed computers and technology and determined this career path was right for me. Unfortunately, after about six months at IBM, I decided that I did not enjoy computer programming as much as I thought I would. So here I was, unhappy with my career choice and ready to search again for another option.

I did some soul searching, trying to determine what I wanted to be when I grew up (even though I was already partially grown up). I have to admit that it was not until then that I realized that every other part-time job I had ever had (with the exception of my CS internships) were in *libraries*. I had worked at my high school library, at the local public library, and at the small library in my dorm in college. Huh, maybe I should look into a career working in a library!

So, that's exactly what I did. I learned that I would need to get a master's in library and information science in order to become a librarian, so I enrolled in the graduate program at the University of Texas at Austin (while I continued to work at IBM). I was pleasantly surprised by the courses that were directly applicable to technology in libraries. Two years later, I graduated with my master's and had decided that I really wanted to work with technology in a public library. My job search began again, and I ended up beginning my new career as the Head of Systems and Technology at the Novi Public Library in Michigan.

Not long after, I realized that I had found a career that fit me perfectly. I was able to help people use technology in a library setting. It was the year 2000, and computers were definitely a mainstay in many libraries by this time. Internet access was a common service, and teaching information literacy was becoming a key role for libraries.

During my five years at the Novi Public Library, I helped the community become more computer-literate, and the library offer more technology services. I was involved at the front lines of using technology to provide library service by developing the library website, providing reference service to patrons, and teaching information literacy classes. One of my favorite classes to teach was on evaluating information on the Internet. During this time, it was common for people to learn how to create a website, and so they would type up any content they wanted and publish it to the Web. At the same time, people were learning how to find information on the Internet and they would often believe everything they read on the Internet to be true. So it was a great opportunity to try to teach patrons how to properly evaluate the information they found on the Web, including the availability of oceanfront property in Michigan! Even today, this remains a skill that is often overlooked.

I spent the next six years of my career as the IT Manager (and later Associate Director) of the Rochester Hills Public Library (also in Michigan). As the IT Manager, I supported the library's integrated library system (ILS), which included a migration to Polaris in my first year there. I oversaw the circulation and technical services departments, as well the few part-time IT staff members.

By this point, technology was becoming integral to everything in the library. We redesigned the library's website and put together a web-based intranet for staff. We customized the ILS to meet our community's needs. We migrated the servers to a virtual server environment. We supported and updated the telephone system. We upgraded the wireless network for the building. We added new self-checkout machines, computer and print management software, and kept the computers up-to-date.

During that time, I encountered many patrons who had a variety of levels of comfort with technology. One day, I was called out to talk to a patron who had requested to speak with the "IT person." This particular patron informed me when I introduced myself that he was an "IT expert" and therefore wanted us to change the way we had things set up on our public computers. Immediately I knew we would never see eye-to-eye. First of all, I never considered *myself* an IT expert (or an expert at anything for that matter). And secondly, this patron had his understanding of how technology works, and yet I knew more about providing technology services for the public, including all the security and privacy concerns that needed to be addressed. In the end, we agreed to disagree, but it was yet another lesson for me in working with the public.

In addition to working with the public and the IT staff on our many projects, we also had to include training for library staff on all the new things we were doing. Technology in libraries was changing rapidly, and patrons were expecting *all* library staff (not just the IT staff) to be knowledgeable about how it works. E-books and e-readers were popularized, but the system for checking out e-books from the library was complicated.

Most importantly, I found that I was in my element, from a career perspective. I loved learning about the new technology and discovering ways that technology could help meet a need in a library. Technology meets library needs in a variety of ways – right there is the key to success. It can be hard to stay focused on that, as one might be tempted to try out all kinds of new technology, just because it's new and cool. However, I learned that technology is only as good as the solution it provides.

After about four or five years at the Rochester Hills Public Library, I expanded my role to that of the Associate Director. I found I enjoyed administration of the library as well. As a leader in the library, I could help staff embrace the new technology and funnel their enthusiasm toward new technology services. I published a book titled *Implementing Technology Solutions in Libraries* with Information Today, Inc., which outlines more directly my approach to technology projects and how I found success in the exciting field of technology services in libraries.

I feel very blessed to have my current position, which is the Director of the Orion Township Public Library in Lake Orion, MI. I strongly believe that my technology background provides me with the perspective needed to be a library director in the 21st century. After all, libraries *are* in the technology business. They provide computer hardware, software, wireless access, and mobile apps for patrons of all ages. Library directors must understand the influence of technology on libraries and how libraries can embrace the ever-changing world of technology.

Typically, I don't give myself any extra credit for being a woman in the field of technology in libraries. That could just be my personality, as I strive to expect only the best from myself and from others, regardless of gender. Men and women alike must be involved in technology in libraries in order for the future of library technology to be successful, which I believe is true for any other industry as well. There are many women employed by libraries, often more women than men. However, there may be more leadership roles in libraries held by men than women, and there may be more technology positions in libraries held by men than women. As both a library leader and a technology advocate, I hope to see that level out, as I believe both men and women have roles to play in libraries and in technology.

For me, I started out in technology and then became a librarian. When I started my professional career in libraries 17 years ago, most technology staff were "techies" who just happened to work in a library *or* librarians who just happened to take over the technology tasks. It was rare to find someone like me who studied technology and libraries and found it was a perfect marriage of careers.

As I look to the future of libraries, I strongly believe that library leaders must also be those who embrace technology. If there is a gender bias in the field, it must dissipate. We must all work together to find ways that technology can provide solutions to needs in our libraries. Patrons walk in the library door today with technology in their pockets. In fact, many patrons do not walk in the library door at all, but simply access library services via their technology devices. Libraries must be able to speak to that technology.

On the other end of the spectrum, many libraries serve patrons who do not have computer technology at home. Broadband Internet access does not exist in every community. Libraries play a very important role in bridging the gap in these communities. Information and technology literacy are critical skills in today's world, and libraries can provide services to help patrons achieve success.

My hope for the future of libraries is that residents across the globe recognize this technological role that libraries play in their communities. Libraries are much more than books. Libraries bring communities together and use technology to help improve literacy skills. Leaders in libraries need to further this vision by sharing their library's services throughout their community and consistently offer services that further their community's needs.

Blending Liberal Arts and IT: Finding a Place for a Tech-Loving Non-Programmer

Amanda Hartman McLellan

#CareerPath #FindingYourPlace #LeanIn #NeverGiveUp

Growing up, I was fortunate to have always had a computer in my house. Even before I could read well, and computers were DOS based, my dad would play computer games with my brother and me, reading out loud the command line interface options to games like "Landing Party[1]" and letting us decide our fate. I grew up with personal computers, and they grew up with me. I spent hours playing games and typing up assignments for school. We had somewhat early access to the Internet, with a louder-than-necessary-there's-no-sneaking-online external modem. When it came to computers, I was taught to be fearless; in high school, my dad helped me build my own computer, and said "You break it, you fix it." I broke it. He helped me fix it.

---

1   Thanks to the good folks at the Internet Archive, you can play Landing Party in your browser. It's not quite as fun as I remember it being. https://archive.org/details/msdos_Landing_Party_1989

I learned to type, in no real thanks to many years of computer lab time with typing tutorial software, but because chatting online was hard when you were henpecking. The required computer course during my senior year of high school spent the first several weeks covering typing. I raised my hand, and asked the teacher "Since I know how to type…" and looked around the room, somewhat incredulous that there were people who DIDN'T know by this point "…can I please work ahead?" Not willing to expend precious energy on an over-achiever, the teacher and principal allowed it. So, a friend of mine and I completed the whole semester course, with the extra assignment of teaching ourselves Microsoft Access, in a quarter. We spent the rest of the semester across the hall in our sanctuary, the art room.

Technology had always been a big part of my life without ever being noticeably that big of a deal. It came naturally to me, and despite my best efforts to ignore my predilection for technology, it always managed to pull me back in. I went to college to study art history without any real plan on what I might do with that degree. Fortunately, I enrolled at DePauw University, so my liberal arts education exposed me to many different disciplines and areas of study. My first year, I enrolled in a computer programming class to fill my math/science requirements. While I passed, it was primarily because of a fantastic professor and friends who helped me understand everything past "Hello World." This class in C++ was the first interaction I recall having with technology that didn't come easily.

However, a difficult computer science class wasn't my only exposure to technology. When I enrolled, I had been invited to join a new program called "ITAP", or "Information Technology Associates Program", aimed to combine technical skills and knowledge with a liberal arts education. I was among the first class to complete all four years of the program. It gave me the foundation with different aspects of technology, hands-on experience, and the confidence to succeed outside of the college classroom. The program is set up to provide on and off campus internships. This means you are doing real-world work, as well as learning the soft skills such as interpersonal communication and teamwork. Through ITAP, I learned the basics of web development, video editing, managing hardware, and marketing. By my senior year, I was teaching the first-year students web design basics, and it was through ITAP that I completed a 5th year internship working as a web manager at a local board game store. The four years of college seemed to have flown by, and I wasn't quite sure what I wanted to do next. My mother had just lost her battle with cancer, and I was feeling very directionless. Through my internship, I knew I didn't want to be a web developer full-time, as I missed the allures of academic life and I wanted to use that shiny new degree in art history. During a lunch with my academic advisor, she asked if I had ever thought to utilize my interest in technology (that was obvious to her but still not to me!) and become a librarian. She had worked closely with the librarians at DePauw to put the art history slides online so that students could better see and interact with the artwork, and she knew that technology was a very important aspect of librarianship. It had not occurred to me, so her suggestion sent me on a path that led to my career.

I enrolled at University of Illinois at Urbana-Champaign with the intent to focus my degree in art librarianship. I obtained a graduate assistantship in the History, Philosophy, and Newspaper Library, where I was exposed to digitization of print material. It wasn't until my second semester of graduate school where I finally assessed my interests and skills and realized I had been ignoring my true passion all along – I was interested in the technological aspect of librarianship. I took mostly information science classes, and embraced my geeky techy side. I took on a couple of additional graduate assistantships dealing with web design and federated searching, and through my coursework I learned a lot about digital preservation, web technologies, metadata, and organizing and finding information. I even tried my hand at learning programming again. This time a Python course. It still didn't come naturally to me. I discovered usability as a concept and fell in love with the idea of blending the technology with the persons using the technology.

After graduate school, I worked for a community college in Virginia as a Digital Services Librarian. I learned so much about reference and customer service, and spent time redesigning the website and becoming involved with local groups of librarians interested in technology. While working there, I also had the great opportunity to teach an introductory technology class, where I taught students how to use Microsoft Office. The biggest thing I learned in teaching those classes and working with my patrons is that my early exposure to computers and technology is a gift that I had taken for granted. Many people, especially those who are returning to school after having worked for several years, or those whose economic backgrounds didn't allow easy access, were so unfamiliar with technology that it was a huge barrier they had to overcome in order to succeed in college. I loved being able to help them learn to be more comfortable around computers, and watch their confidence grow as they learned. I left the community college to work as the Head of Special Collections and Digital Initiatives at Longwood University, and now to the Head of Applications and Digital Services at East Carolina University. I also am exceptionally fortunate to be an Adjunct Lecturer at my alma mater, the University of Illinois School of Information Science, where I teach "Introduction to Technology for Library and Information Science." Every semester, my objective is to introduce basic concepts of technology as well as library specific technologies, and to give my students a toolkit to go forward and build their own pathways for their careers. I explain it's just as important to find what is NOT a good fit as it is to find your passions.

My interest in technology was something I tried to run away from, but it kept bringing me back. Since I'm not interested in programming, I thought there was no place for me in the technology world. Unfortunately, aspects of our culture can discourage women from exploring technology roles. This has had an impact on my willingness to work past my own insecurities. Once I learned that there are many roles, especially for people like me who have cultivated bridging technology with the larger picture, I have finally found my calling. With my students and patrons, I attempt to break down barriers and fears regarding technology – my role as instructor or librarian is to make information accessible and approachable. As a woman in technology, I can help provide mentorship and pathways to the next generation of librarians and information professionals, as active thanks for the many mentors I have had along my path.

If I had a time machine, and could have a conversation with my younger self, I would tell her to embrace her interests. Just because one is not terribly interested in programming doesn't mean there isn't opportunity. It's not all ones and zeroes, it's not all regular expressions and compilers. There's creativity, customer service, usability, design, wonderment, frustration, and teamwork. There's the joy of working with brilliant colleagues and those moments where your support helps your student or patron understand something they previously didn't. Embrace who you are, embrace the opportunities offered, work hard, and then give back. Sometimes you won't be taken seriously, because of your age, your gender, or on rare occasion, because of your lack of a doctorate, but stand up for yourself. It might not always be the easiest path, but it is the one that will make you feel best about yourself at the end of the day.

How Hamlet Helped Me Become a Library "Techie"

Este Pope

#CareerPath #Code #Confidence #DigitalLibrary #Techie

In 1998, I took a college English class called Hamlet in Hyperspace, which considered the influence of technology on the written word. I've never stepped away from thinking about how technology impacts information since. In addition to readings and essay writing typical of most English courses, we also learned how to code HTML in this class, and created our first websites as part of a final project. You might say that we were doing Digital Humanities, but no one was calling it that back then. I titled my website *The delicate web* and had a lavender spider web pattern as a background. The page included "links I like" such as nytimes.com and marthastewart.com. This was 1998, mind you, so the web was a little bit of a different place back then, but still a rabbit hole in which you could get lost for hours. I was a religion major. I didn't really see myself as a "techie" in any real sense. One of the things I did discover from learning to code HTML is that this technology stuff wasn't as mysterious as I thought.

I decoded other technology mysteries while I had a graduate fellowship fixing computers in the Chemistry department. I didn't know anything about taking apart a computer or defragging a hard drive, and I remember feeling distinctly female and somewhat out of place in that job. I found myself wearing more neutral clothes so as not to stand out, and neglected to mention I was studying theology, because then how would these patented, million-dollar grant-funded faculty think I could help them with their Simeon email accounts? I learned so much on this job, like how to run commands in Unix, how to image computers with Ghost, and how to troubleshoot daisy-chained SCSI drives in the labs. After two years, I knew how computers worked and could take them apart. Suddenly, my sewing machine didn't seem so daunting to me; after all, it wasn't all that different from a computer, in terms of how machines work. My love affair with technology deepened.

My work in libraries started with fixing computers, where I was the first-line support for a staff of close to 100. I fixed all department computers, maintained all library file, web, and print servers, worked to implement computer upgrades, lab images, new email clients and library systems, and trained everyone. While doing this work, I saw how a library operates, and thought I would like to be a librarian. By 2004, I finished my library degree while working at the library. I moved into a new group in the library while in library school, involved with digital library building. We were a small team of two, and I was asked to investigate a lot of new tools at the time – Dspace, Bepress, DigiTool, and I had the tasks to install, test, batch load files, configure, and document. It was the early days of digital asset management systems and institutional repositories, and I soaked up everything I could from the burgeoning online communities. I learned to code TEI, EAD, and how to write XSLT transformations.

A favorite memory from my early days in learning digital library technologies is a TEI training I attended in New Brunswick, Canada. I ended up being part of a group of five women who bonded in this training course, perhaps because we were women in a class dominated by men. Honestly, I don't remember if that is what started things. After the first day of the week-long training, this group of women had dinner and connected. By the end of the week, we'd had dinner each night, talking and laughing a little loudly each day as class began. We must have sat in the back row of the training, because we were known as "the back seat girls." What started as an intimidating week of technology training by myself in another country became an empowering and delightful experience of bonding with a group of women doing somewhat similar work. I wasn't alone in this technology work, and it was fun.

My career has taken me on many twists and turns. I've deepened my library technology skills as a systems librarian. During years when I served in more "traditional" library roles in public services and management (without active technology work), I always found my technology background to be an asset. My systems understanding helped me with problem solving. I found that being conversant in the language of technology and coding enabled me to more deeply understand and ask the right questions as I worked on various teams and with departments. Having a technology background also gave me some authority and confidence, which at times added the little boost I needed to advocate or request changes in the library.

Now I'm back in the world of digital library building, and delving deeply into digital repository systems gives me a lot of joy in my work. I love to see technology enable us in libraries to bring our treasures to a broad audience online. I think a lot about my earliest glimmers of interest in technology and information during my Hamlet in Hyperspace course, where I considered the ethical and philosophical questions about humanity and culture, and how technology is a part of, and is transforming, the traditions that libraries support and preserve in society. We are confronted with the challenges of a networked infrastructure in everything we do, and as librarians, we seek to preserve the scholarly record of our time. It is evident that the digital world and technology pose threats to preservation, even as technology is what will likely help us keep a record. I have sitting on my desk the book I read in college, *The Gutenberg Elegies*, still a relevant reflection on reading in the digital world by Sven Birkerts, as well as a new volume edited by Phillip C. Bantin *Building Trustworthy Digital Repositories*, looking at how we ensure survival of our digital content for posterity. Technology has given me tools to do great work in libraries and it is an inspiration, even as we grapple with the many challenges technology brings to our society.

As a woman, I'm not sure I ever thought of myself as less capable of being a "techie," but perhaps in some subconscious way I was intimidated by technology, or thought it might be boring. The opposite has been true for me and I wear the title of "techie" with a lot of pride. I'm not sure I would have arrived at such satisfying work had I not found that Hamlet in Hyperspace course in college, because I needed a way to connect my technology work to big questions about history, society, meaning, and culture. And thankfully I have continued to make those connections throughout my career, and wield the technology powers to hopefully leave this world a little better, and more preserved and accessible.

Chimera in the Library: A Journey Through the Cultures of IT, Libraries, & Library IT

Stephanie Walker

#CareerPath #Advice #DontFearFailure #Flexibility
#HighlightStrengths #HireGoodPeople #Lessons
#ListenToEveryone #NeverTalkDown #ServiceMatters
#SoWhatIfItHasNeverBeenDone #TrustStaff

In library IT, you may undertake formal studies toward a career path. Alternatively, you may find yourself in IT roles accidentally: you weren't afraid to tackle technology, so people turned to you. The latter seemed prevalent in library computing's early days. A colleague of mine tells of being a system's only male librarian twenty-five years ago, and being thrust into the role of Head of Library Systems. He believes gender was a factor. I wish I disbelieved him, but I've often been there from the other side, as the sole woman and manager in a tech environment. Some clients demanded to see the boss, saying "You can't be! You're a girl!" My calculus professor said "girls don't belong in STEM." Computer science remains male-dominated. "A lot of computing pioneers – the people who programmed the first digital computers – were women," writes Steve Henn, in *When Women Stopped Coding*. "But in 1984 ... the percentage of women in computer science flattened, then plunged, even as the share of women in other technical and professional fields kept rising."[2] In 2013, women were "26 percent of computing professionals and just 12 percent of working engineers."[3] Library science is about 80% female/20% male[4] (with men in about 40% of leadership positions[5]). Then there's me. I've often done things in non-traditional ways, and my career is no exception. A chimera is (mythologically) "a monstrous creature with parts from multiple animals" or (genetically) "a single animal organism with genetically distinct cells from two distinct zygotes."[6] I've frequently felt like this 2-in-1 creature, in IT and libraries. I vary my communications from tech-heavy discussions with sysadmins to user-friendly language with those less comfortable with tech. I'm a self-described "tekkie." I'm also an "artsie" – the "other" group on my undergraduate campus, and supposedly, never the twain would meet. Yet I'm comfortable in both worlds. I came to IT by countermanding expectations–beginning when many women departed, then appearing to retreat by joining a female-dominated profession, but taking IT roles. In doing so, I've fostered award-winning organiza-

---

2 Steve Henn, "When Women Stopped Coding,"October 21, 2014 8:54 am ET, in *Planet Money: the Economy Explained*, produced by NPR, audio, 4:33. https://www.npr.org/sections/money/2014/10/21/357629765/when-women-stopped-coding

3 Katherine W. Phillips, "Gender and Racial Bias Is Systemic in the Sciences," *The New York Times*, Room for Debate, updated June 11, 2015, 10:46 pm, https://www.nytimes.com/roomfordebate/2015/06/11/nobel-winning-sexism-in-the-lab/gender-and-racial-bias-is-systemic-in-the-sciences

4 Jessica Olin and Michelle Millet, "Gendered Expectations for Leadership in Libraries," *In The Library With The Lead Pipe* (open access, open peer reviewed journal), November 4, 2015, http://www.inthelibrarywiththeleadpipe.org/2015/libleadgender/

5 Ibid.

6 "Chimera," *Wikipedia*, accessed March 27, 2017, https://en.wikipedia.org/wiki/Chimera

tional changes and successes. This is my story, and five lessons I've learned.

In high school, once I could select courses, I chose STEM *and* humanities options. In university, I majored in "co-op" math & computer science, alternating four months of school with four months of work. I worked in Texaco Canada's Management Information Systems unit. Overwhelmingly, my work and school colleagues were male. Did it bother me? No. There were minor issues: the calculus professor, and colleagues who hung posters of buxom women in their office. I hung a poster of a bodybuilder; if they were going to display something unattainable, so would I. They squawked "No regular guy looks like that!" I replied "I don't look like Adrienne Barbeau." Truce – we removed all posters (as intended). Mostly, though, I was well-treated. But the chimera stirred. After two years, I missed humanities. My Texaco colleagues worked overnight for days to meet deadlines for software to help truckers use unstaffed refueling stations. I considered what I wanted from life: this wasn't it. I switched to English, working multiple jobs, including in libraries. I completed an MA and began a PhD, but restlessness recurred. I liked teaching, but not grading. Computers were expanding in libraries. A library career would blend technology and teaching. In 1993, I began an MLS, and took multiple library jobs.

Upon graduation, in a poor job market, I kept my library jobs, but worked full-time IT jobs–system conversion, support, programming, and managing databases of organ transplant information. I convinced the hiring manager that a librarian with tech skills and familiarity with relational databases could learn Oracle. After interviewing applicants, she said "It'll be easier teaching you Oracle than teaching programmers to coax transplant data from busy surgeons." That was my first lesson in the value of chimera-hood. All tekkies *aren't* lacking social skills, but enough fit the stereotype that I got a job for which I wasn't optimally qualified – and succeeded. **Lesson 1: Value the abil-**

ity to speak to non-tekkies *and* tekkies. Customer service matters.

Still, I wanted to be a librarian. I applied for a position at an academic dental library. My technology skills were unusual for 1997 libraries. The dental library still used paper circulation cards; bibliographic records were not linked to physical items. There were three staff – one librarian, two technicians (all female). The assistant dean later told me she reviewed my resume and said "If this one isn't crazy, we're hiring her." **Lesson 2: Highlight technology strengths.** They're increasingly common but still a selling point.

I got the job. I was thirty-one, supervising women twenty and thirty years my senior. Neither was comfortable with technology, but they knew dentistry faculty and students. The first thing I said was "You know more than I do about this place. I know technology, but there's a lot I don't know in other areas; I need to lean on you. We'll work on tech together; for everything else, you're the experts." We instantly became a team. They later told me they'd worried I'd be a haughty tekkie who'd consider them stupid because they didn't "know computers." **Lesson 3: Never talk down.** I stayed 6.5 years, working closely with all-male IT and media units on technology projects.

Over the years, whatever my title, I've always had IT-related roles. In a small college, I worked with the CIO and others on technology projects. In 2005, I became Manager of Collections at Harvard Medical School's Library, eventually also supervising Library IT and Technical Services. My staff nominated me for a leadership award, which I won. My "IT guy" told me I was the best manager he'd had. He said I knew enough tech to understand his work and needs, I knew how to clear paths so he could work without interference, and I trusted him to do the job and only intervened when he needed assistance. **Lesson 4: Hire good people. Trust them to do their jobs.**

In 2006, I became the Associate Librarian for Information Services at Brooklyn College (BC). BC Library's visionary Chief Librarian, Dr. Barbra Higginbotham, was also Executive Director of Academic Information Technologies (AIT). Twenty years earlier, Campus IT and AIT were a single unit. Faculty felt this wasn't meeting their pedagogical needs. When something big happened, like campus networks crashing, academic needs might be slighted. Dr. Higginbotham argued that a) the Library had talented systems staff; b) librarians were faculty and familiar with pedagogy; and c) Campus IT should be split. Campus IT would handle regular IT priorities; the library would expand AIT. When I arrived, AIT was a well-integrated library unit. I assumed liaison responsibilities and established good relations with AIT and Campus IT. When Dr. Higginbotham retired, I became Chief Librarian & Executive Director of AIT. I spent 9+ years at BC, undertaking numerous technology projects. We supported 2300+ Blackboard courses, taught 600+ technology and library instruction sessions annually, developed an online promotion and tenure file system, created a library/IT Entrepreneurship program, and more.

As part of the Entrepreneurship program, we built a resource management system (WIMS), a laptop loan system, an inventory management system, a timesheet system, and more. We shared WIMS freely with CUNY libraries; 7 adopted it. WIMS won the 2010 Ribaudo Award for Technology Innovation; in 2014, we won another. We helped Guttman College build and host their library website. Then came a unique challenge: scanners. A vendor demonstrated scanners designed not to damage book spines. The cost was about $6000, plus annual fees. We didn't like the price or interface. A staff member said "We could design something better for less." My response? "Go!" This spawns my final advice – **Lesson 5: Don't fear the unknown. If someone tells you something can't be done, don't necessarily believe it.** I'd never heard of libraries going into the hardware business. We did, designing a user-friendly scanner for $2000. We presented at conferences and became equipment resellers. We sold 80+ scanners in 18 months, making about $1000 profit per machine. Vendors noticed; some explored licensing our software. If we'd been able to dedicate more time, I believe we'd have made some small waves. Again, AIT and Campus IT were overwhelmingly male; BC librarians were majority-female. Was it an issue? No. We undertook diversity initiatives, but never for women in IT: perhaps that's an area to explore.

In 2015, I became the Dean of Libraries & Information Resources at the University of North Dakota. I oversee several libraries, and work with people in UND's versions of AIT and Campus IT, and the CIO of the North Dakota University System (NDUS–a coalition of 11 higher education institutions). I serve on the Online Dakota Information Network's Board. Again, I'm bringing new technology projects to a library system, and my dual nature is handy: I speak to people with wide-ranging technology skills. Translating among those worlds is crucial, and my skills "between worlds" are exceptionally helpful. UND had a very traditional library structure, and had not moved into offering the (often technology-heavy) services that characterize many modern academic research library systems. However, a Provost hired in 2013 saw a strong need for change. Retirements in senior library ranks afforded an opportunity, and the "Director of Libraries" position was re-cast as "Dean of Libraries & Information Resources" with a broad mandate to work across campus and into the community.

Since my arrival, I have reorganized the largest library's administrative structure, to allow us to create strong relationships campus-wide and offer many technology-supported services. I redesigned several positions, and hired key staff such as a Digital Initiatives Librarian, a Social Sciences & Scholarly Communications Librarian, a Metadata & Cataloging Librarian, and a new Web Services Librarian. An Assessment Assistant is forthcoming. I created an Assessment Committee, and began our first major collection evaluation; we contracted with Sustainable Collection Services for reporting, data analysis, and other needs. I created the position of Information Literacy Coordinator, promoted a superb librarian, and gave her a mandate to establish new relationships and work with instructional designers on interactive support for learning. Importantly, I've never forgotten my long-ago boss's words, about it being easier to teach technical skills than soft skills. When I hire or promote people, I prefer other chimeras – people with technical aptitude plus strong people skills – and I invest heavily in training.

I have also established strong relationships in areas where they did not previously exist – another area in which my dual skills helped. For example, I'm the first librarian to serve on the Deans' Council. Because of this, I was able to promote to the deans the idea of research tutorials and embedded librarians to help students strengthen their research skills. We piloted this with the College of Business & Public Administration in a series of required courses. Feedback and assessment showed students learned more about key concepts – and so did faculty! I also serve on UND's new Digital & New Media Working Group, which gave me contacts to facilitate planning a Digital Studio in the Library. I also established UND's first Open Educational Resources (OER) Committee, and invited a broad spectrum of participants, including faculty, student government representatives, instructional designers, librarians, and the Directors of the Center for Instructional & Learning Technologies (CILT), the Office of Instructional Development (OID), and the Office of Extended Learning (OEL). We secured start-up funding from the state, then ongoing funding of $100,000 annually from student government and the Provost. We developed a program of workshops, marketing, and technical and research support for OERs, jointly sponsored by CILT and the Libraries. UND's OERs program is now a state leader; we saved our students over $3 million in just two years. We've now begun building an institutional repository, working with faculty, NDUS IT, the Computational Research Center, and CILT. As well, we're reaching beyond campus, working on digital initiatives with community partners. UND Libraries now have a much-strengthened profile, in technology and beyond.

Interestingly, we've seen changes in terms of women in library IT (and IT generally) here. In my past positions with library technology or IT, staff were largely male. As noted, I was often the lone female. In 2015, UND's Library Systems unit was all male. With one promotion and one departure, we seized the opportunity to redesign the unit and add a position. Our mostly newly-hired unit is now 50% female. So are UND's brand-new CIO, the Director of CILT, and the Director of OEL. Perhaps we're making progress after all.

#Challenges

BREAKING STEREOTYPES AND MEETING CHALLENGES

Cathleen S. Carstens

#Challenges #AtMyAgeItsImportantToBeHavingFun
#BreakingStereotypes #ChangeAgent
#ExcitedAboutTheNextGenerationOfWomen
#LifelongLearning #LookingTowardTheFuture
#TechnologyIsInMyDNA

I'm a sixty-year-old woman in a medium-sized suburban public library. I manage fifty-eight computers for both staff and the public. The public network is a desktop virtualization system. I have been in this position for well over eighteen years, having started here on January 3, 2000. I have worked under four different library directors and one interim director. I have been lucky to have a lot of support from all but one of my directors.

When I first started, on January 3, 2000, the learning curve was pretty steep. I soaked up everything I could like a sponge! This sometimes took a lot of forbearance, because my main support person was very difficult to work with. He said himself that he was "no teacher," and he tended to lose his temper easily and frequently. However, I think he treated everybody that way, and did not treat me differently because I am a woman. He moved on after a few years, much to my relief!

I learned from experience, from asking questions, and from any training I could get. I feel that I have been pretty successful, on the whole. The way I got into this position is a result of years of trying to get into a library system that had job security, good pay, and benefits. I live in a rural area where jobs are scarce, so even though I commute sixty miles each way, it is worth it.

I am very lucky to be able to work flexible hours. If I need to reboot servers or do other work that can best be done when the library is closed, I can do that. As long as I work at least 37.5 hours per week and am here for my reference desk shifts, I am not held to a rigid 9-5 schedule.

I am what has been called an "accidental systems librarian," but I look at it as a happy accident. One reason I was originally hired was that I had previous experience with the Novell networking system, which was what the library was running at the time. I have also been exposed to computers nearly all my life, as my father was an engineer who worked with some of the earliest computers.

I also enjoy breaking stereotypes. One, being a woman systems administrator, and two, being of the age at which I am supposed to be unable to learn about computers. I don't feel that I have been treated differently because I am a woman in IT, but it may just be that I don't notice or care if I am treated differently. My life experience has taught me that men won't necessarily treat women respectfully, so I have had to develop strategies for getting what I need and letting the rest roll off my back. What I mean by this is that I am sometimes treated disrespectfully, and sometimes male IT workers treat me like I am ignorant. Sometimes they can be arrogant, thoughtless, and inconsiderate. So I developed strategies such as disregarding body language and tones of voice that many would find offensive. In addition, I try to show interest in them as people with lives outside their jobs. I also present myself as someone who wants to learn from them. I suppose that this could be interpreted as flattering their egos, but if that's what it takes to learn how to manage Active Directory or the right way to reboot the server for our virtualized desktops, I will do it. And I have to add that I have also worked with male IT workers who have been respectful, helpful and professional. I suppose that when you take a cross-section of any profession, the personalities will mirror humanity as a whole. Some people are delightful to be around, and some are difficult.

I don't actually have to deal with male IT workers in person all that often anymore. There is a company hired by our town that supports our staff network, and I have had to work with them occasionally. Otherwise, the male IT workers I see or talk to are usually on the telephone.

To me, a bigger problem with being in library IT is that it is so isolating. I am the only person on staff whose primary job is to manage our IT needs, and I have often wished there was someone who really understands what I do. Our current director is very supportive, as is the staff, but over the course of over eighteen years, there have been many times when someone would make a comment about my "playing on the computers," as though what I did wasn't real work. Or the times I was waiting for something to reboot, and there would be a comment about how I "wasn't doing anything." And of course, there are the times when someone would ask for help, apparently thinking that I could somehow magically solve their problem in a minute or two. There seems to be a lack of understanding in regard to the time it takes to analyze a problem, find a solution, and implement it. I have learned not to be frustrated by these situations, but just try to juggle multiple priorities as necessary.

I like to tell the story about the elderly lady who had a computer that had locked up. I would have to restart her computer, and I was afraid she would lose the document she had been working on for the past hour. She looked up at me and said, "Isn't your systems person here today?" I looked down at her and said, "I am the systems person." A lot of other patrons within earshot already knew me, and by this time some of them were laughing out loud. But the elderly woman persisted, saying, "Oh, I thought it would be a young man." Nope!

My job is structured so that I also spend about half of my time on the reference desk. This has often presented problems, and has led to a great deal of juggling of tasks. A dramatic example of this occurred one terrible afternoon about ten years ago. Our first wireless network was being installed by an outside vendor and I was busy with reference. I kept running back and forth between the reference desk and the area where the installer was working. If I was talking to the installer, one of the librarians I worked with at the time (she has since retired) took it upon herself to find me and scold me for not being on the desk. Luckily, the installer didn't really need my help or company. He could see what was going on, and came to the reference desk when he had a question and when he was finished. He did a fine job, and we used that wireless network until the town built a new library building.

He was almost finished when things suddenly got much worse. My mother called to ask me to find out if it was true that my cousin's son and only child, Jacob, had been killed in Iraq. I used the computer at my desk instead of the reference desk to try to search military websites. This was both a reference question and a personal matter, and I did not want patrons listening to that particular reference interview. Of course, this resulted in more scolding from the librarian who only saw that I was not at the reference desk. I didn't bother trying to explain the circumstances to her because I was pretty sure that she only wanted to make her point and didn't want to listen to any explanation. I was not able to immediately find confirmation that Jacob had been killed, but within a few days family members were contacting each other with the sad news.

When I started, my workplace was on such a rigid schedule that leaving the reference desk to work on a computer was a real problem. I have learned a lot more about time management since then, and now I can put out several fires at the same time. I have also become much more knowledgeable, and can make repairs or perform procedures much more quickly.

One of the things I really like about this job is that it is always different, and I am always learning. It can be like a roller coaster, but with the downs come the ups. When a complicated procedure works, or a patron or staff member achieves a goal, it is incredibly rewarding. I believe that you don't know when you are up if you haven't been down, and the contrast makes the happy times that much better.

I also teach computer skills, and have a program doing individual instruction. Most of my students are beginners who just want to learn the basics. Seeing the happiness they express when the computer finally works for them makes me happy too. I know that I am helping people in a very concrete way. In addition, teaching has helped me to understand just how complicated and sometimes frightening computers can seem. Sometimes they seem like an alien creature that speaks a different language and demands a new set of unfamiliar skills in order to make them do your bidding. And even then, they do things that seem inexplicable. I spend as much time reassuring my students that they are not going to break the computer as I do teaching them to hold the mouse or type in a URL. It has been as good for me as it has been for my students. I have made many new friends, and learned to be patient and far more understanding than I ever was before.

There are also group computer classes, and several of my colleagues and I help with these so that each participant can get as much individual attention as possible. I am lucky to have many colleagues who are very technologically literate, and are also excellent teachers and presenters.

I would also like to debunk a common and oft-repeated myth: the belief that senior citizens are reluctant and have difficulty learning about computers. This may be true for some, but I have helped many men and women well into their nineties learn to use computers, tablets and smartphones. They have learned to do effective internet searches, create Excel spreadsheets, download e-books, audiobooks, and other materials from the electronic catalog, and much more. One of the first seniors I worked with wanted to look up women with whom she had worked as a nurse in World War II. Some of those who are now considered senior citizens helped invent the original computers, and they are perfectly capable of learning to use and enjoy the devices we now have.

I don't know about other branches of librarianship, but as far as I can tell, public libraries seem to have a lot of women system administrators. It seems to be accepted as the norm. In the future, however, there will have to be extensive changes. For one thing, the IT responsibilities should not be a part-time job, with the rest of the job including reference, collection development, or other traditional library work. The IT librarian position should be recognized as having enough responsibilities to be full-time. In addition, the IT person should not be a paraprofessional who gets the IT role thrust on her. This is unfair to the poor person who soon finds herself doing two full-time jobs. The IT person also shouldn't be plucked from the ranks of librarians, unless she has experience or a degree in computer science. The IT person needs an understanding of the unique needs of the library, while also understanding how to manage a network to provide a balance between access and security.

The way things have evolved in our library has worked out very well. As I mentioned above, we have a number of librarians who are adept with technology. As a result, we act as a team, with me as the person who specializes in technology and makes final decisions. We collaborate on technology training, maintenance of the desktop virtualization system, and other aspects of library technology.

Librarians graduating today are really knowledgeable about technology. Much of what we have now didn't exist when I graduated with my M.L.S. in 1991! Library technology can be a big challenge, but the rewards are many.

Our library is doing its part to encourage young women to consider a career in IT. As I write this, we are holding our first session of the Girls Who Code program.[1] I am not involved with it, except for making sure that we have the necessary network capacity. The young librarian who is running it seems to be having a wonderful time. Whether these girls go into library IT or not, they will bring about one of today's most needed changes as they remedy the gender imbalance in IT. They will use tools that have not even been invented yet to create a marvelous future for all of us.

---

1   *Girls Who Code*, https://girlswhocode.com/

EMOTIONAL LABOR: THE UNEXPECTED HARD WORK

Tara Coleman

#Challenges #EmotionalLabor

As the Web Services Librarian, I provide leadership in the co-ordination, organization, maintenance, and assessment of the libraries' website. I am responsible for ensuring consistent branding and identity management across all aspects of the Libraries' web presence. The hardest part of my job is not coding, creating and editing text, or providing a positive user experience for our patrons. It is the emotional labor required of me to be successful at my job.

I came upon the term emotional labor in a blog post and I quickly fell down the internet rabbit hole to learn more about it. Articles in The Huffington Post[2], Jezebel[3], The Guardian[4],

---

2   Christine Hutchison, "Why Women Are Tired: The Price of Unpaid Emotional Labor,*" HuffPost The Blog*, April 6, 2016, https://www.huffingtonpost.com/psyched-in-san-francisco/why-women-are-tired-the-p_b_9619732.html.

3   Tracy Moore, "Is it Even Worthwhile to Teach Men to Value Emotional Labor?," *Jezebel* (blog), November 15, 2015 (3:15 pm), https://jezebel.com/is-it-even-worthwhile-to-teach-men-to-value-emotional-l-1742222786.

4   Rose Hackman, "' Women are Just Better at This Stuff': Is Emotional Labor Feminism's Next Frontier?," *The Guardian*, (November 8, 2015), https://www.theguardian.com/world/2015/nov/08/women-gender-roles-sexism-emotional-labor-feminism.

and Everyday Feminism[5] explained a feeling that I had trouble articulating to others. Emotional labor is the expectation that people, often women, will cater to the needs of others with a smile and sympathetic ear before themselves. It's being emotionally aware, likeable and kind, regardless of how you really feel or are being treated. Essentially, it is regulating your feelings so that others around you feel good and have a positive experience. All of this is done without reciprocity or financial compensation. To be clear, I think that being friendly and having a sympathetic ear is a very important part of customer service. However, it becomes a challenge when it feels like there is a greater expectation for women to do this than men.

My work focuses on the main library website, but I am often the first person contacted when people have questions, want changes, or have concerns about something they see online, regardless of whether it falls under my purview. This is understandable. My job title has the word web in it and it makes sense that I should be able to answer questions about anything on the web, be it the intranet, databases, or our discovery tool. Some come to me because I am visible in the organization and easy to access, some because they know I will explain information in a way they will understand, and others because I make them feel like their question or request is important and that they are not stupid for not already knowing the answer. If I feel that someone is not comfortable bringing a problem forward to the right person, I often bring the problem up myself. I know the personalities in my organization enough to know when and how to bring up a problem so that people are not on the defensive, though that is not always avoidable, and I am willing to listen to someone vent or complain if they are.

---

5 Kai Cheng Thom, "8 Lessons That Show How Emotional Labor Defines Women's Lives," *Everyday Feminism* (Blog), June 15, 2016, https://everydayfeminism.com/2016/06/emotional-labor-womens-lives/.

The most challenging thing I do to be successful is to advocate on behalf of others in the organization. I believe a common mistake people make is assuming that others understand and believe the way they do. People who work with the public may believe that a tweak to the search algorithm is an easy way to help confused patrons find what they want in a discovery tool or database. Their lack of experience in programming may lead them to believe something is less complicated or time consuming than it really is. They likely do not have an idea of the consequences one tweak has towards other parts of the tool or what will happen when the product is upgraded. People who work in IT may not understand the magnitude of the issue because they do not use the public side of the product daily, nor do they have frequent contact with upset patrons. It can be easy to say that patrons should behave differently or that the issue is not a big concern.

If you start with that assumption, it is easy to get angry when things are not done the way you want. That anger can become a barrier to communicating with others and getting things done. I am often in the position to explain that public services is not stupid if they ask twenty times why a particular function cannot be done with our discovery tool or that IT is not lazy for not switching to a new discovery tool when the one we have does not provide a particular function.

I believe that you do what is necessary to do to get work done. Sometimes that requires taking extra time explaining why we cannot use certain colors on a webpage to get buy-in from a department head, or stroking the ego of a programmer before telling them to stop making "cool" changes to the website. However, catering to the feelings and concerns of other people is exhausting. It is particularly exhausting when I do not see men inside or outside of library IT putting in the effort I do.

When I make this observation people often say that I am just a better communicator and that I have good people skills.

That is true. I value those skills and work hard to be good at them. Some people believe when IT guys are not good listeners or when they talk above people's heads it is because they are wired differently, which is what likely drew them to the profession. I have a different opinion. I think people generally associate patience, good interpersonal skills, and effective communications with women, and many people associate IT skills with men. As long as organizations allow men to get away with having fewer interpersonal skills, women will continue to carry the emotional labor in library IT.

If managers want to change the culture in their departments and more equitably distribute emotional labor among the staff, they can start by setting an expectation for a certain level of behavior and interpersonal skills and modeling it themselves. Pay attention to how work is distributed and who is contacted more often. If the person bearing the brunt of the emotional labor is anyone like me, they may not realize it at the time. It can be helpful if an authority figure steps in and asks others to step up. If a member of the staff is hard to communicate with, there should be an expectation that their communication skills improve, and consequences for not doing so. Changing to a more equitable work culture can be difficult, but once achieved, it will improve the work lives of everyone in the department.

YES, I SPEAK TECH; MY EXPERIENCES WITH SEXISM IN THE WORKPLACE

Suzanna Conrad

#Challenges #ExperiencesWithSexism #RisingAboveSexism

I debated a lot about whether or not I should submit my experiences to this book. Often when I attribute any misfortune I've had to my gender to my friends or family, I am (mostly by male friends or family members) greeted with the sentiment that I am being too sensitive. I am unlikely to share these kinds of experiences about sexism with my coworkers or professional colleagues, especially with male colleagues, as they might be perceived as weaknesses. The problem is that there is no clearly defined line for what is or is not sexism in the workplace, because you cannot know what another person is thinking with his or her comments or actions. If someone has said something that I perceive as inappropriate, are his or her motivations based on the fact that I'm a woman, experiences of interactions with me, or is this just normal behavior for this person regardless of gender?

It's also not easy to call someone out on sexism. Some people are sexist without even thinking and would vehemently deny that they behave this way. This includes women. Studies on search committee perceptions of female and male job applicants are a perfect example of how sexism affects both of the sexes when hiring academics.[6] Salary gaps between men and women in the U.S.[7] perpetuate sexism. Women are judged for working, not working, having children, not having children, and many other personal choices where men face less scrutiny.

The experiences I'm describing in this essay are not exclusively limited to those from library IT, where I now work. I worked for a decade in the mobile gaming and applications industry before transitioning to libraries. Sexism has exposed itself in some form in almost every position I've had, whether for a corporation or a library.

About Me

I am the Head of Library Information Systems at Sacramento State University Library, a position I began in September 2016. Prior to that I was the Head of Digital Services & Technology / Digital Initiatives Librarian at Cal Poly Pomona. I have an MLIS from the University of Illinois, Urbana-Champaign, an MBA from University of East London, and a BA in history from Cornell University. My journey to library IT was a backwards path; I've always been interested in web development and at any given time maintain a number of personal websites or websites for family. I don't have any formal IT training beyond the data curation specialization from my

---

6   Toni Schmader, Jessica Whitehead, and Vicki H. Wysocki, "A Linguistic Comparison of Letters of Recommendation for Male and Female Chemistry and Biochemistry Job Applicants," *Sex Roles*, 57(7-8), (2007) 509–514. http://doi.org/10.1007/s11199-007-9291-4; Juan M. Madera, Michelle R. Hebl, and Randi C. Martin, "Gender and Letters of Recommendation for Academia: Agentic and Communal Differences," *Journal of Applied Psychology*, 94(6): 1591-1599, (2009).

7   Kevin Miller, "The Simple Truth About the Gender Pay Gap," *Economic Justice AAUW*, Spring 2017, http://www.aauw.org/research/the-simple-truth-about-the-gender-pay-gap/

MLIS. Most of my technology experience is practical – I have an aptitude for systems and technology and have, because of this aptitude, been given various projects that are technology focused at many of my jobs. At my first job out of college as an office manager, I developed a secure customer portal and assisted with network issues. I've managed websites for my employers whether through a content management system or editing using HTML or text editors. In 2004, I started working in the mobile gaming industry and as part of my work in business development and product management, I frequently interacted with or managed development teams creating mobile content. In 2009, I worked in the electronic games industry for a little under a year.

During 2009, I decided I needed a change in the focus of my career. I had been working for profit-centered corporations since 2001 and I wanted a career that contributed to the public good. After some soul searching, I enrolled in the MLIS program at University of Illinois, Urbana-Champaign with the intention of working in an academic library, perhaps due to my experiences as a student assistant at Cornell. I was interested in technology in general, but also digital archives. My first job as a librarian was at a public library configuring a city documents database, followed by a temporary job at Guitar Center as a taxonomist/search engine specialist. In 2012, I was hired at Cal Poly Pomona as the Digital Initiatives Librarian. My search for a full-time academic librarian job had been challenging; it was rare for me to receive phone calls for systems or emerging technologies jobs, since often they required knowledge of very specific library systems. I still have the attitude that any system can be learned if you have technological aptitude – job descriptions and search committees did not seem to share my confidence as I was invited for very few interviews in systems departments. Cal Poly Pomona was really the only institution where I was called in for a systems job interview. All my other interviews were related to scholarly communication or licensing; I had an internship for the Data Curation Toolkit Profiles Program at Purdue, so I seemed to fulfill some basic scholarly communication requirements. I don't believe that any of my challenges in finding a job were related to my gender, rather lack of positions and restrictive job postings asking for very specific, very academic library centric traits.

I have had a few mentors and supervisors that have provided career progression guidance and tips for managing others. I had one supervisor in a public library internship that was technologically savvy and provided guidance on what classes I should take during my MLIS, but not as many tips for landing academic jobs. At another internship for Purdue, I discussed the interview process, professional development and publishing with my supervisor, who provided valuable feedback and tips. I cannot recall any other mentors that worked in IT or were exceptionally technologically savvy. I did not have any mentors from my time in corporations, but to be fair those kinds of relationships are rare and have to be actively sought after. It's not as simple as my position at Cal Poly Pomona where they assigned me a mentor upon hiring. I had heard about some mentoring relationships that male colleagues had in my corporate experience, but mobile gaming and applications development were male dominated industries; I was frequently one of the only women in the room. I don't attribute the lack of mentorship in the corporations I worked in to gender, rather the competitive nature of those corporations not being conducive to these kinds of relationships.

I Am a Woman, I Probably Don't Understand Technology Much

In 2008 I was hired by a start-up to acquire and integrate content in a mobile application that was marketed in emerging countries. The goal of the application was to give customers access to information services via text messaging. In many emerging markets, this was a beneficial innovation at the time; many did not trust the network charges associated with using GPRS[8] and were more accepting of services using text messaging or SMS.[9] I had been in the mobile applications industry for four years. I had a comprehensive understanding of how wireless carriers, our main partners, structured revenue sharing agreements. I was the only woman in a team of four full-time employees, including the CEO, a product manager, and a VP of Sales. My predecessor had been an MBA student with an engineering degree, but no experience working with wireless carriers or mobile content. When I went into my interview, the CEO hesitated because I didn't have enough "technical experience" compared to my predecessor, who had worked in software engineering and product management for the shipbuilding industry. The requirements of the job included working with content providers in U.S. and remote markets to implement feeds (API, XML, or even automated CSV ingests) by wireframing suggested solutions and talking to our developers to make sure content was integrated effectively. In my prior job, I had managed development projects for mobile games, implemented a vendor-supported e-commerce platform for delivering content, and managed our online portfolio. Arguably, my experience was far more targeted and relevant than that of my predecessor.

Years later, when working in systems at an academic library, I was the library contact for centralized desktop support. One IT manager with whom I was in frequent contact would dumb things down for me. The library was submitting a grant application to purchase tablets for the classroom and I was charged with budgeting technology costs. This IT manager had recommended Windows Surface Pros and for grant submission, we had included Pros with i3 Intel Core processors at his rec-

---

8   GPRS is data for 2G and 3G mobile phones.

9   Short message service.

ommendation. Months passed and we received the grant. In the meantime, i5 and i7 models had become available, which changed our budget drastically. At this point, he told me we had to purchase i7 models in order for them to be supported by campus IT. I was trying to find a solution to purchase some sort of device, whether it was Windows Surface Pros, iPads, laptops, or something else that would allow us to have at least 30 devices and stay relatively on budget. In our discussions, rather than listen to my problem – how do I buy 30 devices with warranties that meet IT's minimum standards for service – he spent time explaining processors to me in analogies. For instance, "I tell my 5-year-old son that there's a difference between a minivan and a Ford Mustang – you won't have the same horsepower, so you can't go as fast." I was aware of the differences between the processors we were considering and was mindful of the need to have devices that IT would support; I did not need an introduction to processors talk (I'm going to also pretend to ignore the comparison to his son. While I love children, being told analogies appropriate for youngsters does not make one feel particularly well-respected professionally). This was not a solitary experience with this IT manager; there were at least five instances where his "intro to computers for dummies" left me frustrated and questioning *his* professionalism.

So I can complain about not being taken seriously or having my technology skills doubted, but what do I do about it? The best advice I have for any woman (or man) in IT whether in a library or anywhere else is to communicate effectively. Don't pretend to be an expert in things you are not an expert in. I admittedly do not know much about the actual ins and outs of desktop support, despite supervising a desktop support person. I can weigh in on user perspectives and the importance of customer service. I also rely on staff in my department to be the experts on server administration; they rely on me to make connections and keep communication flowing. There are some people that have preconceived notions about your skill levels or competencies whether based on sexism or not. The best that you can do is try to communicate well with them.

Another tip is to desensitize yourself from bad interactions or criticism. I do not expect the IT manager I described above to ever take me seriously, and because of his behaviors, I don't take him seriously either. That's OK. There are other people who have a lot of respect for me and my technological skills. Getting defensive in these situations or trying to justify your own skills makes you look worse rather than better. I sat in a meeting one time with a web consultant, who when confronted with our criticisms of the approach for a web redesign, stated "I've won awards." Touting your own achievements defensively does not make you look particularly collaborative or portray you in a positive light. Desensitizing myself doesn't mean I don't notice or acknowledge bad interactions, rather I evaluate whether or not I can do anything about the situation. If so, I think about an approach for resolution. If not, I try to let it go and concentrate my efforts on more positive situations.

I Am a Woman, I Am Most Capable of Administrative Tasks

At a startup I was working for, I was asked to take notes during meetings. We had a part-time administrative assistant who could have attended meetings and taken notes. At first I complied. I have always been a team player; I generally frown upon people with the attitude that they are too good to occasionally do the grunt work. That said, others should be team players too. None of the men were ever asked to take notes. After a few meetings with me taking and sharing notes, I suggested that we trade off note-taking duties each meeting. All the men refused. After this happened, I had an honest discussion with my then boss, the CEO, about what my real priorities were and how concentrating on those was a far more effective investment for the company than me taking, editing and sharing notes while others at the same level of the organization refused to complete the same work.

Despite this conversation, I had a run in with one of the company's investors. First, the investor and I had already had friction. He had attended a few meetings about strategy and had made some suggestions regarding our content plans that were not feasible technologically – he wanted to create an "app store" of sorts on our application. Since everything communicated via text messaging and not GPRS, I tried to explain that there was no way to download apps to the phones via SMS. I also mentioned that maintaining a complete portal of purchasable content was complicated and would require a lot of infrastructure (note: I had launched one of these portals with a major company only a year prior). He was not particularly thrilled with my criticism of his ideas. After this interaction, there had been a meeting to discuss strategy for getting the application on a specific hardware vendor's phones. Since I was responsible for content in the application, not the devices on which the application must run, I was not included in the meeting. They had jotted down notes on an easel pad. This investor carried the easel into my office, plopped it down, and said "Suzanna, write up the notes for this and send it to me." And he left. Our part-time administrative assistant was in the office at the time and was confused that he had not carried the easel pad to her, as she expected to be asked to take minutes. I was not sure what to do – on one hand, I had already clarified the inappropriateness of being the sole minute taker in a room full of men who were supposedly at the same level by discussing the issue with my supervisor. Nevertheless, it seemed bad form to rock the boat with an investor. Ultimately, I determined that when you let one inappropriate instance slide, more would result. As a compromise, I took a picture of the easel pad with my phone and emailed it to the investor with a polite and brief message about how I was very busy working on content contracts and negotiations to make the application a success. I CC'd my boss. Unsurprisingly, the investor did not take it well; he responded with threats to fire me and that my insubordination would not be tolerated. My boss stepped into the email conversation and informed me that I should continue working on my actual priorities as I had suggested. The investor never addressed me directly again despite frequent trips to the office. I was assured by my boss later that the investor had only contributed a small amount of money and that he was not concerned about our interactions. I wonder if he would have had the same reaction if the investor would have been a major one?

My suggestion for combating sexism where your duties are notched down because of gender is to prove your own competency and to not be afraid to approach people directly to resolve issues. When I discussed the note-taking issues with my supervisor at the startup, while I probably could have, I did not talk about gender. I talked about equal distribution of work and our priorities. My priorities were to meet content integration goals, not to take effective minutes at meetings. When comparing myself to my male peers there, I talked about our job duties, not our gender. I did not complain publicly about the note-taking, I just addressed the issue with my direct supervisor and resolved it very quickly. I tried the same route with the investor by trying to bring his attention to my actual duties and job description, but whatever preconceived notions he had of me were not easily shattered. So in that case, I could only indicate facts in a professional manner with him: "my priorities as determined by my supervisor are X and in order for the organization to be effective, I have to keep doing X and not Y." Could I have gotten fired? Potentially. Luckily for me, I had proven my worth in the organization already so it never came to this.

What Can I/You Learn?

It's hard to combat sexism without being called out for sensitivity. I have the impression that women are expected to take on what are considered male characteristics: be tough, don't show emotion. I feel that if I am tough and unemotional, I will be more respected. It's also very hard to avoid imposter syndrome when you're a woman in IT without an IT degree. Dominique

Bortmas from University of South Florida gave a great presentation at Code4Lib 2017 about imposter phenomenon. In the results of Bortmas' survey, women consistently ranked high on feeling intense, frequent or moderate imposter phenomenon.[10] Certainly, recognizing that you fall victim to imposter phenomenon and self-doubt is important. Bortmas has some great suggestions for combatting your own tendencies toward imposter phenomenon – I particularly like the recommendation to do "positive feedback reflections." I think of this as mini "pep talks" to myself to remind myself that there are reasons I am where I am that are not solely a result of luck. It has been difficult to find permanent positions in librarianship for years. Attributing luck to someone getting a new, challenging position discounts their drive and achievements.

Mentorship continues to be important for combating sexism in library IT. Both women and men need to serve as mentors to new faces. Mentees should be actively aware that they can get help and advice from other professionals. Mentors can give one perspective about different ways to approach a situation or brainstorm solutions. We all also need to start sharing. I shared these experiences in this essay with a former colleague who was amazed that these situations had happened to me. We should be aware of all our alternative realities and have empathy for one another regardless of our gender.

Summary

Fortunately, I have had many experiences in and outside of libraries where I feel that my professional contributions were appreciated. I have not felt that I've been passed over for projects,

---

10   Dominique "Dom" Bortmas, "Destroying Imposter Phenomenon in Code4Lib and Ourselves" (presentation, Code4Lib Conference, Los Angeles, CA, March 7,2017), https://drive.google.com/file/d/0B1ZWw7jPvbGfcE1KTGZmT0Qwd3M/view.

promotions, or new jobs because of my gender. And that's what really matters – knowing that my efforts have and will continue to be rewarded. I don't want my story to dissuade anyone from considering a career in IT. I have found that working in technology can be very rewarding with unique challenges and opportunities. Good communication and honesty about your own abilities is what can help one succeed in the field.

Empowerment, Teamwork, and Personal Growth

Deloris J. Foxworth

#Challenges #Empowerment #ImposterSyndrome #Strength #Teamwork

Several years back I held one of the most exciting jobs I've ever had. After earning a master's in library science, I joined the Scott County Public Library (SCPL) as the technology manager. This role was not only interesting and fun, but it was also empowering. For starters, I was only the second person to hold this role at SCPL. Second, I was the first woman to hold this role. What made me feel most empowered in this role, though, was the variety of tasks before me. Many would find this overwhelming, but not me. This was my time to learn, my time to shine, and sometimes even fall flat on my face. The position was both challenging and very rewarding.

I remember one of the first tasks put before me: investigating the malfunctioning coin machine attached to the public copier. The library staff warned me this was a constant issue as patrons inserted coins too quickly, inserted random objects besides coins, inserted ripped bills, and more. Heeding the warning and knowing the IT contractors for the library could not help with the coin machine, I embarked on my first adventure.

I was a little nervous, okay, a lot nervous! Had I ever taken a coin machine apart? Was I mechanically inclined at all? Not really, but I did not let that stop me. Growing up, I never felt like I could not do something mechanical because I was a girl. In fact, my dad even made a point to teach me and my sister how to change a flat tire and use jumper cables (I did the latter multiple times).

Back to the coin machine: opening the casing, I was not quite sure what I would find, and more importantly, unaware of how to put it back together if pieces started flying upon opening. Much to my surprise, nothing came flying out. It was actually a quite simple machine once I got it open. There was an overflow bin for coins at the bottom, a coin sorter at the top that hid the return lever, and the circuit board that made it all work. All of these pieces were removable, allowing me to explore the crevices of the machine. Fortunately, I had long fingers and small hands so I was able to explore the machine. Upon investigation of the smaller crevices I found the problem and removed the debris on the coin sorter that was keeping the coins from entering the correct slot.

I was feeling great. I fixed the coin machine. Now, only one thing remained. I had to put all the pieces back in place and get it to work correctly. Ugh! This was truly nerve-racking. Taking things apart is not that challenging, but putting them back together, now that's another story. Summoning all the confidence and mechanical knowledge my dad had instilled in me, I started putting it back together. With each attempt, I got a little closer and a little more frustrated. I was determined not to give up. And it paid off, I finally got it back together and operational. Most importantly, I did not break anything. What a relief!

This experience early during my time at the library was very instrumental in building my confidence and a relationship of respect among the other library staff. This act confirmed to many, including myself, my place and value among the staff and organization. The staff now looked up to me as a problem-solver and as a technology wizard, although I found that to be a bit of an exaggeration.

From that experience, I went on to tackle problems with the employee copier, public printer, WI-FI connections, patron devices, and more. As I continued to build my confidence with technology and mechanics I eventually tackled bigger projects like programming the security door locks and moving and setting up new computers. While these may seem like no big feats at all, they were huge to me.

The door locks required a lot of investigative work to start as there was no instruction manual and the library's computer equipment had been updated, but the door lock software had not. The security software would not even install on the new computer operating system. Not giving up and determined to make this work, I corresponded with the manufacturer and the library's IT consultants and ultimately found a way to get proper software installed. Then, after learning how to use it, I was able to remove and add security codes to the employee entrance and program the door.

By this point I was feeling pretty good about myself, even though much of the work I had completed with assistance. I had definitely gained the respect of my co-workers and patrons who had attended my technology trainings or interacted with me otherwise. However, none of this would prepare me for the issue I was about to face.

As a respected leader at the library, I was tasked by the director to work with outside contractors to construct and install a remote kiosk and library locker system for patrons out in the county. I met with both the building contractor and the kiosk and locker salesperson multiple times throughout the project. While we encountered a few minor setbacks like weather and a delay in delivery of equipment, those challenges were no match for what I was about to encounter.

The construction was complete, the equipment had arrived, and it was time to install the equipment in the building.

This is where the first truly significant test of my confidence came in. The kiosk had been set up and now it was time to install the lockers.

They did not fit! I had been in charge of my first major project for the library and I had failed.

After investigating, I discovered I had used the wrong equipment measurements to guide the construction of the building. Oh, what to do? My mistake was going to cost the library substantially more money and delay the opening of this location.

Frustrated, the building contractor agreed to make modifications to the building. However, before the work began, the kiosk and locker salesperson had another idea to try, but he would need the building contractor and the technology contractor's help. Working into the evening, the newly formed team found a solution.

My nerves were a little shaken. How would I face the library director again?

The library director and I met on site the next morning and the newly formed team came through. Despite the error, the installation looked fabulous. No one could even tell there had been a problem.

I was relieved. My director continued to call on me for tasks, and more importantly, she did not mention it again. The mishap did not change her perception of my work.

I continued to work on technology projects and conduct trainings for the library. I even managed the remote location and trained new staff how to use it. After about a year, the library was set to construct a second remote system. I was once again tasked with overseeing this project. Nervous, but determined to do it right this time, I worked with the same building contractor and equipment salesperson. I know they were nervous working with me again, but I think I proved myself. I carefully worked with both of them to make certain we had the correct measurements for the equipment and that the building would fit completely around it. When this project was done, it was evident I had at least partially redeemed myself in the building contractor's eyes (he was the one that doubted me the most). More importantly, my confidence improved and I had learned and grown through both experiences.

Sadly, my time at the library was cut short as I was determined to embark on a new adventure. Since then I have made even another job change. However, I will never forget the lessons I learned and the power of positivity I held as I tackled new projects every day and completed most of them successfully. Sure, I had a few mishaps, but don't we all. The important thing is I kept going.

Most importantly, I learned that true empowerment stems from working with great people, male or female, who not only appreciate successful work, but also understand and support the challenging process of individual growth.

My Life in IT

Lynne E. Grigsby

#Challenges #CareerPath #Discrimination #Sexism
#UnconsciousBias

I have been in IT since the early 1980s, but began in a unique way. I started out in a typical "female" job as a receptionist in a new department called the Division of Library Automation of the University of California, Berkeley. I had been extremely lucky to work with this new group of programmers and librarians who were breaking ground with building Melvyl, the union catalog of the University of California. The atmosphere was what many would describe years later when talking about dot coms. It was full of young people who were doing things that hadn't been done before.

I didn't have any programming skills, but I was young and curious, so I took a Pascal class. As the group was growing, I quickly moved from receptionist to overseeing the receptionist and other administrative staff. Recognizing my increased responsibilities, my supervisor worked to have me reclassified as a "data analyst," but it was continually blocked. The university's reclassification review group didn't really know what a data analyst did. To allow me to move up, a manager suggested I become a programmer, as I had done well in my Pascal course. It was an easy reclass, and likely to go through.

I was willing, and started learning PL/I, the programming language of Melvyl. When the reclass came up for approval, I took a couple modules I had written, showed them to the reclass group, and my reclass was easily approved.

I was now a programmer/analyst working on a mainframe with both men and women, who were programmers, computer operators, librarians, and analysts. The work was interesting. The job environment was collaborative and open. Most of the time.

Unfortunately, a couple of women didn't accept me as a programmer. They continued to treat me as a secretary and called me for things, no matter how many times I told them my job had changed and whom they should call. As a young woman in my 20s, I was shocked that they were so unwilling to accept my advancement. Not all women, but a few, made the job transition harder than I had been expecting. These same women had always been supportive of my moving up administratively, but this transition to programming seemed to have thrown them. Over the years I have stayed in contact with them. If I told them this, I am sure they would be surprised and disagree with me, as both identify as being supportive of women.

I got used to being in meetings with just one or two other women. I got used to being called a "guy's gal" because they felt I talked to them like a man and not a woman. (What does that mean?) I got used to being called Xena when the TV show was popular. I got used to being ignored at conferences.

At work, I found that if I wanted to grow and be pushed technically, I had to ask for new assignments as they often went to the one man on the team. In spite of all this I thrived and continued to move up.

I now manage the library IT unit at the UC Berkeley Library. I have hired people who ended up being surprised I was a programmer, could understand what they were talking about, and didn't want euphemisms. I also can't tell you the number of interviews with male candidates who won't look at me or respond directly to me. They look and angle their bodies to the men. My lead technical person is a woman. During an interview, while addressing the technical staff, a candidate waved at all the men and ignored both of us. Interviewees are told I am the hiring authority, but after the interview they call my boss, a man, not me. One called to tell him he had another job offer. I told my boss to tell him that he should take it.

After such interviews, I have talked to the men in the room and they have rarely noticed what I have. Rarely have they noticed to whom the candidate addressed his answers.

In my personal life, I did dog rescue (taking dogs from the shelter, fostering them, and finding homes) for 10 years. When talking to people, we almost never discussed what I did for a living, but when we did, the looks of shock and amazement always caused me to pause. Why were they surprised? Was it that I was a woman? Or they couldn't believe I had another job?

That is part of the problem with sexism — it can be subtle and we often grasp at other reasons. Was it sexism or are we being overly sensitive?

I have three sons. When they were younger and I was out with them, I can't tell you the number of times I got sympathetic comments from female strangers. Not because they were misbehaving, but because they were three boys. Whenever I met a woman who was the mother of three girls I would ask her if she got the same sympathetic comments. They all told me never.

I notice how few women around my age have let their hair go grey, and also notice how many men have. Why? It is easy to blame it on ageism, but are men less affected or worried about it? Does that make it sexism?

We can spend hours, and too much energy, on debating if slights are real or imagined. We can't always know the intention, but we can work on how it affects us and what we do in response.

I try to mentor young women I meet or who work for me. One of the things I tell them is to speak up for themselves. Men are more likely to ask for what they want, and they should do so too, as no one is going to ask or advocate for them. I talk about asking for the money they think they deserve, not just accepting what is offered. I talk about work confidence and knowing the value of your work — I try to separate this out from personal confidence and self-worth as they are two different things. I also talk about taking on new work challenges, and volunteering or asking for what they want. I also tell them not to be afraid to feel stupid. When you have been doing the same thing for a long time, it is easy to be confident about what you know. With a new project, the unknown can be scary. I tell them to think about what they would tell their friends in the same situation, not what they tell themselves.

However, I don't tend to mentor the young men. Is that sexism?

FEMINIST FINDS HER FOOTING

Dana Haugh

#Challenges #CareerPath #ChangeAgent #Sexism

I came into library IT in a kind of roundabout way. I majored in English during my undergraduate career and had aspirations of becoming either a novelist or professor or something of the sort. I was also working part-time as a circulation clerk at my local public library, and though I enjoyed what I did, I never thought I'd make a career of it. Post bachelor's degree, I realized my idyll lifestyle (living in Stars Hollow, writing the next best fantasy novel, teaching graduate English courses) was not in my immediate future and I needed to find a full-time job, any full-time job, as quickly as possible. I had a tiny bit of marketing knowledge from an internship so I put my excellent writing and communication skills (thanks, English degree) to work and landed my first full-time position as email campaign coordinator.

I worked in the company's web department with three men, effectively giving me my first taste of the gender imbalance that seems to plague IT related areas. My supervisor was exceptional, patiently teaching me how to code image-based emails, enlightening me to the various marketing nuances, and encouraging me to build simple websites to expand my design and development knowledge. I took these skills with me to my next position as a web manager at a smaller (again, male-dominated) marketing company. I had more jurisdiction to expand and refine my web development skills but my co-workers were particularly terrible. Every day there was at least one sexist joke or demeaning slur directed at me. By my third year in the marketing industry, I'd had enough. Late one Sunday night I decided to apply for my master's degree in library science.

I completed my MLS in just over a year and was offered a full-time job at the academic library where I worked during my master's program. Since the library department was located inside the institution's innovation lab, I was able to incorporate basic graphic design into my role as materials and acquisitions librarian. I was also able to write for the lab's online publication and utilize some of my drawing skills for the publication's cartoon commentary section.

Fast-forward a couple years and I was able to land my ideal position as web services librarian at my current institution. For me it's the perfect mix of design control, web management, and traditional librarianship. The position is challenging, the workplace support is exceptional (and respectful), and I thoroughly enjoy coming to work every day.

Counting Down to Looking Up

Rhela Sudo

#Challenges #Bias #Sexism

I originally wrote this essay with a lot of anger and resentment towards my experiences in IT over the years. I wanted to tell the reader how recently it was that subtle and not-so-subtle sexism existed in IT, as well as management practices that would not be tolerated today. I also wanted to tell the reader about experiences I've had or seen with women in IT, where it seems that women undermine or degrade each other just as much as men. I have worked through the anger. I have realized part of my frustration was that "back in the day," I did not know what to do in those uncomfortable situations. I did not know if I was justified in feeling uncomfortable. I did not know whether these situations were considered inappropriate by the workplace, even if I felt that they were inappropriate. I did not know if there were resources or policies available to help me handle these situations.

I was afraid to speak out back then. Writing these vignettes is my way of speaking out now.

Twenty-five Years Ago: Corporate IT

I remember walking into a coworker's cubicle to ask him a question about permissions on a certain UNIX directory. I saw a disturbing flash of cartoon blood, tentacles, and female body parts on my coworker's screen–what I later found out to be the Overfiend rape scene from Urotsukidoji. My coworker promptly switched to a new full screen terminal window, whirled around and looked at me blankly. I said, "uh, never mind, I'll check the man pages". "Man pages" is sort of programming slang for "manual" or documentation. The phrase could also sound like a male slur or innuendo. I guess at the time I tried to deflect the awkward incident with sarcasm. This incident happened over twenty years ago. I certainly wouldn't call this incident harassment, but it sure made me uncomfortable.

Twenty-two Years Ago: Corporate IT

I remember another incident where another female coworker and I walked into a male coworker's cubicle. I made sure to knock this time. The male coworker's secondary monitor displayed a video loop of a bouncy pair of breasts – possibly a screensaver? He turned around and asked us how he could help us. The breasts still bounced behind him. We both stammered, and pretty much forgot the question. We said, "We'll come back later or contact you on chat." The breasts still bounced. The male coworker said "Sure thing, let me know if you need any help with anything," and turned back around to his desk. The breasts still bounced. My female coworker and I walked away, dumbfounded. We agreed the guy was a creepy pervert and avoided him from that point on.

Twenty Years Ago: Corporate IT

I worked a contract job at a now-imploded corporation. My department head was always looking at pictures of Harley's on his Mac, so I felt safe in that hopefully I wouldn't see any more tentacle porn.

My direct supervisor was a different story. She told me that since I am a young starry eyed woman, I'd better get serious right away with my work, or I would not last in this environment. I replied that I understood; I will work as hard as I can.

Every time I received a phone call, opened a desk drawer, turned in my seat, my supervisor would pop up... all six feet of her. She'd stick her head up over the sea of cubicles and look around to see who made the noise. She was diagonally across from me, so she'd peer right over me and glare down.

I did a lot of Freehand, Photoshop, ActionScript, Macromedia Lingo, Flash, and HTML work. I took the projects that no one else in the department wanted to do. One coworker did not like doing Photoshop retouching, so he gave me all his retouch work. People were very impressed at what I did, including my department manager. My supervisor learned of this, fumed and told me, "Well, your Freehand skills aren't up to par, so you need more work on that." So, my priority projects became Freehand package labels for the next few months.

The department manager left town for several weeks on work travel. My supervisor told me, "no personal phone calls; keep all work calls to a maximum of two minutes." I didn't feel comfortable enough with other coworkers to ask them if this was true or something arbitrary. The problem: I received a lot of international and interdepartmental calls. I was building computer based training material for the company, in addition to the 'priority Freehand package labels.' Often, there was no way I could keep the calls at two minutes. My supervisor called me into her cubicle and criticized me for length of phone calls. Again, she brought up her opinion that I am a "young inexperienced woman who talks too much and is not serious enough for a job of this magnitude." I said that I will recommend that all vendors or people I work with need to email me from now on, and walked out.

Fifteen Years Ago: Corporate IT

I had another tense experience working in a different, yet slowly imploding company. My boss there was a woman. She told me right away, that she did not like sneaky people or people fresh out of school. I wasn't 'fresh out,' but I didn't want to argue the point. I said to her, "I understand. I would request anything I needed or had questions about directly."

My work environment felt like a time travel nightmare to middle school, circa the 1980s. My female coworkers constantly criticized (but occasionally complimented) my hair, clothing, even my eyebrows. I tolerated this at first, but gradually found this intrusive and rude. When I needed to ask one of these women a question, they'd put on their headphones as I approached them. So I stuck to using email.

My boss would occasionally call people into her office, close the door, and yell at them. Even from several cubicle labyrinths away, and no matter how loudly I cranked up the music on my headphones, I could still hear her yelling. She did this to men and women. I would see people walk out of her office looking shaken and embarrassed, and then go right back to their cubicle to continue working.

Back then, I was not brave enough to ask anyone about this behavior. I knew it was unprofessional, but who was I to say anything? I was a newbie to this company. I was afraid. Looking back now, I feel that the isolating cubicles and hierarchy of the company created a culture of fear.

About a year and a half into this job, I found out about a project within another department of the company that no one had the skills to do. In a multi-departmental meeting, I said I could help with the project – I was familiar with Flash, Action-Script, and Shockwave for developing technical animations of product functions. Now, Flash is deprecated and avoided, but back then it was 'the thing.'

I discussed my ideas and experience with several people in that department, and they wanted to bring me on board. I had no idea how corporate culture worked regarding sharing people across departments, bidding on time, Human Resources involvement, etc. I admit, I just wanted to code and help build good stuff.

So, the other department bid for me to work half time there, and half time would be at my original department. Well, my boss would not have any of this. She called me into her office, closed the door, and screamed. I blanked out and heard mostly screams, no content in the screaming. The only thing I remember clearly was her accusation that I was the sneaky student she thought I was from the very beginning. I don't remember my response to her, nor what else she screamed afterwards. I do remember leaving her office shaking, and throwing up in the restroom.

Fortunately, the President of the division of this company advocated for me and the department that requested me. I endured my boss for the remainder of my contracting stint, because of the engaging work I did and was respected for during the other half of the day.

Four Years Ago: Library IT

One of my worst experiences was at a library technology conference. I was new at my job in an academic library department. I hoped to get perspective from other attendees, who were mostly female. Many seemed to know each other already. I am not the most socially graceful person for sure, but I picked up more than the usual 'who's this woman' cold shoulder vibes from the crowd.

I attended a variety of sessions, including A/B Testing, Analytics, Digital Archiving, and Imposter Syndrome. When I asked questions about library specific 'things,' the resounding answer consisted of glares, giggles, and "why am I here if I don't know this stuff?"

There was a call for lightning talk presenters. Not many were heeding the call. I thought maybe I could put together something about a project I just finished that was integral to our library. Maybe that would earn me some respect points.

The audience response consisted of dismissive quips such as: "This is so convoluted; couldn't you have just used the cloud?" (My answer: "No, because we needed cross domain access."); and disbelief: "Our organization has an entire web team to do this work; how could you do this alone?"

(My response: "We have very little funding and I am 'the coder' in our in our department).

My perception as a newcomer was that I was unwelcome, an outlier. IT and library culture promotes acceptance, tolerance, and inclusion. I was married, older than the majority of people there, not a pioneer of anything, just someone new to library culture, but also knew how to program. I came from a corporate and freelance background. I hoped my years of coding "old school" might be interesting to some people. But I ended up feeling dismissed because I wasn't 'hip' enough.

I totally understand that conferences are exhausting and require much brainpower and stamina to organize. Lunch comas, red-eye flights, reservations, AV and technical setup are very stressful.

I believe there needs to be some type of "acceptance of newbies" in library IT world. Library IT is a unique subset of IT. It is a bridge between the worlds of IT, and Library Science. I feel that questions to people new in library IT should be phrased in an inquisitive, rather than dismissive way. Having a background in corporate IT should be considered an asset, not a hindrance.

Two Years Ago: Library IT

I took on a project ensuring that my department's web pages would survive the company-wide transition from an outdated CMS to the latest version. I communicated with the lead developers and did my best to streamline custom code, JavaScript, CSS, edited content, and verified everything was responsive and mobile friendly.

We sent the main IT department wireframes, requests, explanations, demos, and use cases of what we needed. They'd assured us they would accommodate our needs, but didn't. Many things our department needed were not included in the main site redesign, so during a meeting with the main IT department I brought up our department's concerns. One of the men said to me, "Why are you bringing this up? I was on your hiring committee. This is not in your job description." I was stunned. Somehow, I responded: "My powers have grown since I was hired."

I hoped a nod to science fiction would tone the conversation down. There was a bit of nervous laughter from the other people in the meeting. Another person said that I (my department) had legitimate concerns, and then we continued on with our meeting. But I spun on the guy's "…not in your job description" statement for the rest of the meeting. I spun on it for the rest of the day. This guy was also in IT, so it stunned me even more that he would say something like this. IT platforms, software, and code constantly change. IT people are always doing things beyond their job descriptions. Was this a sexist remark? Was this guy being condescending? Was he doubting my abilities? Was he just being an asshole?

2017

A female programmer friend posted a picture of a mug from a convention that said, "Hacker: Penetrating all the holes." She said, "You have to have a thick skin working in majority-male professions sometimes." The mug also had a 5 finger hole grip. I jokingly replied that it looked like a set of brass knuckles, so you could clock anyone who tries to act out the slogan on the mug without consent.

The Ugly, The Bad, and The Good

We have ways to go with sexual harassment and inappropriate workplace behavior, but things have improved over the years. Most institutions and corporations in the US have "Zero Tolerance" policies, sexual harassment awareness training, and "Safe Zones." Women in STEM, Girls Who Code, and other movements have been instrumental in encouraging women to learn to code, learn how to empower and support each other, and also learn when to speak out about inappropriate behavior in the workplace.

I have often wondered why I stayed in IT over the years. I've heard horror stories from women that are beyond anything I've ever dealt with. But I also heard about the women IT pioneers and women in IT who persevered. I always admired women who stuck it out in IT years ago, when computing as we know it was in its infancy. Perhaps I wanted to prove that if they can do it, I can do it too. Perhaps it was survival – I needed to earn a living. I believe the main reason is simple and almost cliché: I love to code and solve problems. IT is not the only skillset I have, but I am comfortable with computer based challenges – it's the human challenges I must work on, as do we all.

WALKING THE TIGHTROPE!

Sharon Whitfield

#Challenges #Bias #Discrimination

Before I became a librarian, I worked in an information technology (IT) department that supported a community college. I had typical female responsibilities in IT of training and help desk support. Yet, I wanted to transcend those duties. I wanted to use my background in computer programming and start creating. Working in IT, I encountered a highly masculinized department. I was often talked over and kept out of decision-making. As I looked around my IT department, I lamented about the fact that I had no women to mentor me on how to break through a masculinized department or to help me through a career transition. I began to explore other areas and fields of study that would allow me to create. This is how I became familiar with libraries.

I had always hated libraries growing up, which I know will shock many. I found libraries to be a stumbling block to information. I thought libraries were archaic and irrelevant. I found OPACs to be clunky and not user friendly. My feelings were reinforced in the quiet study and no eating policies that I encountered as I walked through the door. Yet, when I volunteered at the Carnegie Library of Pittsburgh, I found a culture shift in libraries was occurring. There were now community spaces and librarians who were embracing technology. I also found the ALA Code of Ethics more akin to how I wanted to behave as a professional.

Entering the library information science program was a rude awakening for me. On the first day of classes, I realized how different I was from my librarian peers. While some of my colleagues did identify social justice issues as a rationale for entering librarianship, others said that they had always loved libraries and books. When it was time for me to speak, I said that I loved technology and I wanted to transform libraries and librarianship.

After studying library information science part-time for two years, I was ready to shake up libraries. I wanted to make communication between librarians and patrons easier. I wanted to make the website more user-friendly and inviting. I have now been a technology librarian in academic libraries for over ten years. I have accomplished some of those tasks by implementing web forms and chat services that makes the library accessible 24/7. I have also created and maintained LibGuides that help patrons find the information that they are seeking faster. In those ten years, I have also seen libraries become more dependent on technology. While I have been able to address access issues at libraries, I find that I have encountered many of the same problems that I faced in the IT department that supported an entire academic institution.

Libraries are gender stratified[11]. Although progress has been made since the implementation of Title IX, most admin-

---

11   Marta Deyrup, "Academic Library Leadership, Second Wave Feminism, and Twenty-First Century Humanism," *Leadership in Academic Libraries Today: Connecting Theory to Practice* (2014): 91.

istrators are still men; most technology librarians are men[12]. I find that gender once again has become an impediment. Looking around the room at any systems/technology meeting, I find that I am the only woman there. My comments are repeatedly ignored until a male colleague reiterates the same comment or suggestion. I am not included in the decision-making process. When I get upset about something, I am perceived to be irrational, but when a colleague who is a man is upset his hostility is considered to be acceptable. Male colleagues will often adopt ideas, best practices and technologies that I have created without any or little attribution. Sadly, I'm okay with this and have learned to accept it because I know that it is a victory to have my idea adopted.

As a woman technology librarian, I also have to conform to the social norms of other female librarians. This often results in my performing a highly technical role, but also a public services role that many male librarians are not expected to do. For instance, in past positions, I have been hired into public service functions and asked to work the reference desk and train my library colleagues when other male colleagues were not.

Our profession needs to be aware of this gender stratification to create more equity and diversity in the library profession. I acknowledge that I am in a gender-incongruent area of librarianship. I walk the tightrope between the masculinized areas of technology and the female dominated areas of librarianship. Yet, as our profession becomes more reliant on technology, what will that mean? Will it mean that library technology will be more highly valued than public services? If technology is

---

12   Ibid.; William Fisher, "The Question of Gender in Library Management," *Library Administration and Management* 11, no. 4 (1997): 231-236; Suzanne Hildebrand, "The Information Age vs. Gender Equity," *Library Journal* 124, no. 7 (1999): 44-47; Lori Ricigliano and Renee Houston, "Men's Work, Women's Work: The Social Shaping of Technology in Academic Libraries," *Association of College and Research Libraries 11th Annual National Conference, Charlotte, NC*, vol. 1. 2003.

more highly valued, will the librarians and professionals be paid higher? If women are not entering library technology, will the women's perspectives in library system designs be considered?

My hope is that in the future, with more women technology librarians entering the profession, walking the tightrope will be easier. Unfortunately, I am not optimistic about the future if women in technology do not work to change it. This is why I urge more women technology librarians to start mentoring and encouraging more women to enter into technology fields, particularly library technology. I know that I was encouraged by a female library science professor to go into systems work even though I felt that I lacked the knowledge to maintain a network.

I know how important it is just to plant the seed that women can enter into technology fields. When I was a multimedia director, I used to take computers apart and have my female students put them back together. My hope was that my female students would not fear getting "techie" and I know it worked for some of those students. I continue to try to mentor women who are interested in pursuing library technology, but our numbers are dwindling. I urge women public services librarians who are interested in technology to consider working in that area of librarianship. It is important that we don't experience the same professional gender stratification that we had in the past where only men were in administration[13]. Let's learn from our past and create opportunity and equity in our profession.

---

13 Marta Deyrup, "Academic Library Leadership, Second Wave Feminism, and Twenty-First Century Humanism", 91; Suzanne Hildebrand, "The Information age vs. Gender Equity," 44-47.

Where I Belong

Becky Yoose

#Challenges #Community #ImposterSyndrome

As I head back from the 12th code4lib annual conference in LA, I reflect on the conversation that I had with a gentleman in the conference elevator during the second day of the conference:

> Gentleman: Is there a conference going on today?
> Me: Yes, there is!
> Gentleman: Women in technology?

That statement caught me off guard. I quickly recovered and said that it was a conference for folks working or interested in library technology. He got off the elevator after my clarification, leaving me alone to reflect on the exchange. Only a few years ago I was joking with the few other women attendees that this was one of the only library-related conferences that didn't have a line to the women's restroom. This year, there was a line at times; nonetheless, a line is a line, and there are a lot of folks that would consider this a success of various changes and initiatives throughout the years.

What changed this attendance dynamic? A code of conduct adopted in 2012, an increase in number of diversity scholarships, broadening the narrow scope of the conference, the establishment and growth of the LibTechWomen group[14] (for women in library technology), increasing awareness among the community about the experiences of being a woman in library technology, and changing actions to become more inclusive–it is the sum of these parts, and more, that pushed this male-dominated community and conference towards more diverse gender representation.

Does a change in numbers really reflect a change in status for women in library IT, though? Library staff are not immune to the greater gender wage gap seen in other professions.[15] The early days of the code4lib community had the trappings of other technology communities with regard to social norms, including sexism and other -isms in group interactions, which caused some women and other underrepresented and vulnerable groups in technology to leave the group or to not join. While the code of conduct and other social support groups have helped mitigate (but by no means fully eliminate) this type of behavior, there is still the problem of Impostor Syndrome (also referred to as Impostor Phenomenon).[16] This year's conference saw a presentation about the prevalence of Impostor Phenomenon in the code4lib community, with women show-

---

14   LibTechWomen, http://libtechwomen.org.

15   "Library Workers: Facts & Figures," *Department for Professional Employees*, AFL-CIO, last modified June 2016. http://dpeaflcio.org/programs-publications/issue-fact-sheets/library-workers-facts-figures/.

16   Impostor Syndrome is when an individual believes that they do not possess knowledge or skills to have achieved their successes, and believes that they are a fraud. (Pauline Rose Clance and Suzanne A. Imes, "The Imposter Phenomenon in High Achieving Women: Dynamics and Therapeutic Intervention," *Psychotherapy: Theory, Research and Practice* 15, no. 3 (1978): 241-247.

ing higher rates of Impostor Phenomenon in almost all demographic categories, including age and length of time in the profession.[17] The library technology community is not immune to the cultural and socioeconomic influences of more general technology culture, particularly in terms of challenges faced by women. Add in the fact that librarianship is a feminized, service profession, and the gender expectations and roles become more skewed.

Coming back to the elevator conversation, perhaps the reason why I was caught off guard was that the data was presented without context and thus can be misinterpreted. The gentleman who made the observation in the elevator was only seeing numbers. Perhaps the gentleman's observation is telling of how we as a community decide what successful change is. Numbers at a conference or in a community can only get one so far. The work done by the library technology community to increase participation by non-male-identifying folks has had some effect, but showing up does not necessarily indicate that those who show up feel like they belong in the community. One of the many hats I wear is a community manager hat, and when I talk to self-identified women in various library technology conferences, I hear similar variations of the same message–"I don't belong here." I keep hearing this year after year in my nine years in the library technology community. I hear this from newer women in the profession, as well as women who have been in the community for years.

That could ultimately be why I was caught off guard by the gentleman's comment. After nine years in the community, I'm still not sure if I belong here.

---

17   Dominique "Dom" Bortmas, "Destroying Imposter Phenomenon in Code4Lib and Ourselves" (presentation, Code4Lib Conference, Los Angeles, CA, March 7, 2017, https://drive.google.com/file/d/0B1ZWw7jPvbGfcE1KTGZmT0Qwd3M/view.

#ChangeAgents

Girls to the Front: What Riot Grrrl Tells Us About Women in Library IT

Kate Dohe

#ChangeAgent #DIY #Feminism #Leadership #RiotGrrrl

I learned about "leaning in" long before Sheryl Sandberg[1] put her manicured hands to the keyboard. Competitive speech and debate gave me my first lessons about smiling prettily when facing a male opponent to avoid appearing "too aggressive." I would lose rounds to girls with thin arguments and short skirts. None of my male squad mates would receive as much unsolicited "advice" about their hair, their shoes, the fit of their pants, or the cut of their shirts as I did by the age of sixteen. None of them were told to invest in a good manicurist because their hands were lovely but their nails were terrible. Debate taught me how to succeed in patriarchal spaces. Riot grrrl—a feminist, DIY punk movement that produced a number of bands, zines, and local communities in the 90s—taught me that the goal should be blowing the patriarchy up entirely. I was too young

---

1 COO of Facebook, and author of *Lean In: Women, Work, and the Will to Lead*, 2013.

for the first wave of riot grrrl bands from Olympia or DC, in a town too conservative for zines or girl meetups. I browsed the "alt rock" new release wall at CD Warehouse in Springfield, Missouri every week, looking for albums by women—this was only intermittently successful, as my old copy of Joan Osborne's *Relish* may indicate. I eventually picked up Sleater-Kinney's All Hands on the Bad One, and subsequently included "You're No Rock & Roll Fun" on every mix CD I ever made for a boy (in retrospect, this was a mixed signal). With more exposure in college, riot grrrl became the lens through which I viewed the world, and it's an ethos I strive to embody personally and professionally. The challenges I've faced in my career aren't found in Sandberg's book, but the answers are in Kathleen Hanna's "Riot Grrrl Manifesto."[2] I have included a few guiding principles from the manifesto to frame my experiences in library IT.

> "BECAUSE we hate capitalism in all its forms and see our main goal as sharing information and staying alive, instead of making profits or being cool according to traditional standards."

I chose libraries over start-ups because the work and the mission matters. I chose technology over reference because I had the skills and knowledge to get things done, facilitate communication, and do my part to make sure our most at-risk digital assets can get to someone else in the future. I am far from a theorist in radical librarianship, but I advocate for openness and DIY as guiding principles in library technology. I believe in repositories, not "proprietary publisher platforms." I want every visitor to our digital collections to exercise the right to read in a private space, not to send analytics back to a parent publisher so

---

2   Kathleen Hanna, *RIOT GRRRL MANIFESTO*, accessed July 05, 2017, http://onewarart.org/riot_grrrl_manifesto.htm. The riot grrrl manifesto was originally published in 1991 in the BIKINI KILL ZINE 2.

they can make "data driven editorial decisions." I recommend the adoption of open-source technology, and support participation in those communities, because I believe that to be one of the most significant ways we can control our own destinies.

> "BECAUSE we don't wanna assimilate to someone else's (boy) standards of what is or isn't."

I struggled at great length with the decision to submit an essay for this collection, because I honestly don't know if I'm "IT" or not. I'm a "digital *something* librarian" by trade and training, not a developer or sysadmin. I can write a bash script or a simple Rails app, but that isn't my job. The language of my post-MLS career has been about sprint planning, scrum meetings, velocity, and backlogs, but if I'm not the one who does the thing, who lives and breathes Eclipse and Pivotal and git commits, am I truly "IT"?

I am far from the only woman who questions my status within a group, and I have spoken to many of my female technical librarian colleagues who struggle with the same identity and expertise questions I do. To my mind, the only way to shut down this source of self-doubt is to stop caring about the question entirely—whether anyone considers me IT "enough" is irrelevant to my abilities, and I would rather bring more people together to accomplish a thing than worry about who belongs at the table.

> "BECAUSE we are unwilling to let our real and valid anger be diffused and/or turned against us via the internalization of sexism as witnessed in girl/girl jealousism and self defeating girltype behaviors."

A few weeks ago I got drinks with some of my former male library IT colleagues, and the conversation turned to the behavior of one of the women we had worked with. One of the men I was with said, "Well, women just always hate other women, that's how it is," and I retorted with "No, *she* hates other women, and that's patriarchy at work. Not all of us buy that bullshit."

I have worked with women in library IT who happily step on the necks of other women to gain attention and approval. This is often subtly done through microaggressions—minimizing the contributions and roles of women in a technology team, limiting opportunities to share expertise, dropping other women from "sidebar" conversations that are relevant to their work, and simultaneously claiming credit for and denigrating another woman's abilities. Some women willingly participate in the patriarchy—lean in—at the expense of women who through economic status, race, disability, or other dimensions, do not present as "professional" (often a term used to reinforce patriarchal, racist, and ableist norms) and may be unfairly criticized. This perpetuation of a fundamentally oppressive system must be called out. In the project-driven world of library IT, this can be particularly problematic as our work is often poorly understood within our organization, and women who are the victims of such tactics may have even fewer options for recourse.

As I said to my former colleague, I don't buy that bullshit, and I don't tolerate it in my teams. In my meetings, I do deploy amplification tactics—calling out someone's idea or contribution by their name, and doing my best to propel the idea forward. I strive to promote the expertise and accomplishments of all my colleagues at every opportunity, cognizant that women inevitably have a harder time being considered experts. I am very sensitive to how often women are asked to talk about their own appearance in the workplace, e.g. the ritual of women telling other women what they like about their attire and personal grooming as a form of small talk. This excludes and alienates women who don't participate in such norms, and is rarely experienced by men. If women are going to succeed in this world, we need to elevate each other and detach from patriarchal systems that encourage us to bully, exclude, and condescend.

Setting Our Values as Library Technology Leaders and Women

Margaret Heller and Hong Ma

#ChangeAgents #Collaboration #Community #Flexibility #Workflows

Our technology department is small. Hong Ma is the Head of Library Systems, which at one time was the only librarian position in the department. She joined Loyola University Chicago in October 2013. She plans and provides oversight for the library's technology infrastructure, and is lead administrator for library systems. Traditionally this role has been the main integrated library system (Voyager) administrator, but she has taken a lead in migrating from the legacy system to a next-generation library services s platform (Alma/Primo), and created a much more collaborative administrative structure. She also works closely with campus IT to ensure interoperability between library systems and campus applications.

Margaret Heller is the Digital Services Librarian and joined Loyola in January 2013. She oversees digital collections and front-facing web services in the library, including managing the institutional repository. Her initial job was to manage the institutional repository and web development for the website and other web applications. This has shifted over the years to include administration of the discovery layer and managing the digital preservation program in coordination with the archives.

We represent a situation not uncommon among library technology departments—a small group who needs to get a lot done: maintaining what is currently in use, implementing new tools and services, and envisioning what will be coming in the future. Beyond that, we are proud that we have created a library technology department that is unusual. There are three full-time staff in the department. Two of the full-time staff are women, and when you include graduate students, at one point we had a department with a majority of women of color. In this essay, we will share some of the highlights of what we have managed over the past four years as the department shifted from entirely male to majority female staff, and how we make it work. Our approaches reflect our own lives and circumstances, and while they will not apply to all, what will apply are the ways in which perceived weaknesses actually created strong results. As part of our values as women, we incorporated inclusiveness within the library and across the institution, initiating projects with participation from all units, cultivating a culture of collaboration by increasing communication in different channels, promoting technology uses, and distributing technology administration roles across library departments. Keeping transparency and trust in our minds, we have been increasingly building our skills of communication, project management and leadership which empowers us to be able to manage most technology projects in efficient and collaborative ways.

In addition to Hong and Margaret, the other full-time member of the department is the systems administrator, who manages the servers, operations, and desktop support. Loyola University Chicago is a private American Catholic research university located in Chicago on two campuses (as well as maintaining a campus in Rome, Italy). Loyola University Chicago Libraries have a total of sixty-three employees including thirty librarians. While the University Health Science and Law schools have separate administrative structures, several items such as the library services platform, interlibrary loan system, and proxy server are shared with one or both other schools and administered primarily by the main library.

Given this situation, the three members of the library's systems department must be very flexible and collaborative to accomplish what they do and maintain the library's technical infrastructure in good working order. It also means that women are taking a lead on technical projects and decisions, and this has led to positive changes in technology at Loyola. The projects that we have worked on are not by any means unique to us, nor are our approaches specifically related to gender. That said, we have slowly changed the approach taken to technical projects in line with our personal and institutional values of care, reflection and openness. We try to cultivate an environment of flexibility and collaboration in order to help all library staff feel more confident with technology.

Moving to the Cloud Thoughtfully

Over the past few years, more of our services have been moving to hosted software. This includes most significantly our library management system, Alma, along with the discovery layer, Primo, which we implemented in 2015. We also have moved more of our tools to Springshare products away from locally developed alternatives. In 2016 we implemented Preservica, a cloud based digital preservation system, and will use the public access module of this tool to replace a locally hosted CONTENTdm. However, we have not, and do not intend to move, all of our infrastructure to the cloud when it is a benefit to maintain it locally. A server of one's own is a powerful thing, and we have the great fortune to have a systems administrator with a close relationship to the campus information technology office. This gives us the flexibility to experiment, try new tools, offer new services, and maintain our independence. We try to move to the cloud when it will be a benefit to us by clearing up time fixing legacy systems or dealing with installing proprietary software, but try to stick locally where it gives us more flexibility.

Increasing Collaboration

One advantage of moving to the cloud on some tools is that they often have sophisticated permissions and user roles built in, so it is relatively simple to give other people levels of access they may not have had before. We believe strongly in the importance of library staff feeling empowered to use technology and solve their own problems without us becoming a roadblock. This approach, in part, came out of necessity. Between the two of us we had three children in three years; Margaret in 2014 and again in 2016, Hong in 2015 (an addition to her twin daughters). The experience of supporting each other and learning to ask for help across the organization through pregnancy, childbirth, maternity leave, and breastfeeding taught the critical importance of documentation, backups, and flexibility. While this helps in our case as working mothers (and our coworker's case as a dog parent), it truly helps the library become better by ensuring that everyone has the amount of access they need to get their job done, and is aware of what everyone else is doing. We have moved almost all our project management to web-based collaboration tools, and standardizing the documentation to increase transparency in our ongoing work. Now if someone is out to deal with family issues but needs to keep up, or has a need to catch up on work while nursing a baby, she can do that. At the same time, with increased cross-training, it means that catching up is less vital since many other people across the library can handle problems.

Becoming User-Centered

While the library as a whole is strongly user-centered, we have tried to increasingly move to user-centered design principles in our technical decision-making (for these purposes library staff also count as users.) In certain areas the systems department had always been very user-centered, but a culture of user-centered design and assessment was something we brought. As women, we are aware that things are not always designed with us in mind, and that understanding helps us look to the needs of others. We started routine usability testing and analytics assessment in 2013. Problems turned up by user testing led to a number of projects such as moving to a responsive and accessible website layout, improvements to our discovery system and link resolver, an overhaul of our interlibrary loan login, and a move to single sign-on for all our web applications (still in progress). By making user testing and feedback a central and early part of all our projects, we make it clear that this is a valued part of our development process.

Automating and Streamlining

Library staff now must all be technologists to some degree, but that does not mean they should have to complete arduous technical tasks or hack their tools to get a useful result. We need to serve their needs and let them focus on their core interests by analyzing workflows and removing barriers where possible. For example, our website layout for years required a representative of the public relations committee who wanted to post a promotional image on the homepage to submit it along with a lot of information to Margaret, who had to hardcode all this into the site. If Margaret was out or busy this could seriously impede the public relations work of the library. In 2016 with the new site layout, this process changed to give the power to the public relations staff member, who now manages her work on her own time and delegates as needed. We followed a similar process for institutional repository collection development.

Conclusion: Keeping a Seat at the Table

The systems department is small compared to other departments in the library. The two of us are major resources for identifying needs, initializing major technology projects, and aligning these projects with the library's strategic goals. Leadership requires risk and pushing forward, but it also requires care and relationship building. In this capacity, we play an essential role in building new partnerships with other campus units. We participate in the Academic Technology Committee to select new tools and contribute ideas about how to get faculty buy-in for adopting new technologies to enhance teaching and learning, and collaborate with the Center for Textual Studies and Digital Humanities to support digital humanities projects. In addition, Margaret recently began serving on the University Senate as the library representative. Both of us pay close attention to new technology trends and their impact on libraries through professional publications and conferences. We both maintain a strong record of service to the profession as well as contributing to professional research and publications. We have been playing active roles in key professional organizations such as the Library Information Technology Association (LITA) and Code4Lib. We have both chaired LITA committees and interest groups, planned Code4Lib conferences, and participated in other boards and committees. Margaret recently was elected to serve on the LITA board as Director-at-Large. We say all this not to brag, but to make a point. We see it as a value to show up and make our voices heard. We stay relevant as technologists, decision makers, and leaders.

GIRLS DON'T DO WOODWORKING

Catherine Larson

#ChangeAgent #Advice #GenderNormsChanging
#SupportingFolks

When my mother was six, she came home from school and excitedly told her parents that she'd been instructed to bring in a block of wood the next day to practice woodworking. Her parents dutifully found some wood for her to use. The following morning, block in hand, she walked into class. In that instant, she learned she was different. "You've misunderstood. This was a project for the boys," her teacher said, "Girls don't do woodworking."

I've had it relatively easy in comparison, as gender norms have changed significantly since that day. I'm able to do things women traditionally were never encouraged or allowed to do, with barely a comment. I've worked for a woman-owned web development business, had both male and female bosses, and worked in industries that are historically male dominated (IT), as well as female dominated (libraries). I've even learned woodworking from a woman.

My family was instrumental in my involvement with computers and libraries. The irony is that initially we had no television, yet computers infiltrated the home. They were tucked in my brothers' and parents' rooms. Over the years, one made its way out into the living room as computers became more ubiquitous. I can still remember watching an animation my brother had created on his Amiga of a cartoon character puffing smoke rings over and over again. As I stood in my brother's room, I was enthralled by what the computer could do. I never gave the location of the computer much thought until recently when I read about "the phenomenon of the computer in the boy's bedroom."[3] Authors Margolis and Fisher surveyed women in Carnegie Mellon's computer science program and though at first it seemed anecdotal, discovered that many women had similar memories of observing their brothers or fathers on the computer. The common theme of woman as observer and man as tinkerer was solidly mind-altering for me.

I may not have had a computer in my room growing up, but I did have my parents' support. Indeed, it was my mother who taught me HTML, just as she had taught herself. My father, thrilled to have a co-conspirator in all things computer-related, also found every excuse to encourage my use of computers. My family's interest and push to involve me in computers clearly influenced and gave me a solid start in my career. As the head of Systems & Technology in my library, I believe I am traversing a gender divide and so I still find myself questioning, "Do I belong here?"

I'm not alone in this feeling. In fact, in 1978, a paper by Clance & Imes, was published on a study that gave a name to this feeling: "imposter syndrome"[4]. Valerie Young elaborated on this paper in her book, *The Secret Thoughts of Successful Women*,

---

3   Jane Margolis and Allan Fisher, *Unlocking the Clubhouse : Women in Computing*, (Cambridge, Mass.: MIT Press, 2002), 23.

4   Pauline R. Clance and Suzanne A. Imes, "The Imposter Phenomenon in High Achieving Women: Dynamics and Therapeutic Intervention," *Psychotherapy: Theory, Research and Practice* 15, no. 3 (1978): 241-247.

where she provides steps to acknowledging that feeling of being found out as an imposter or someone who doesn't belong and recognizing that the work one does truly is because of hard-work and effort[5]. For me, learning that this type of doubt is normal and–for some–expected, has helped me to gain firmer footing in my dual-role of Librarian and Information Technology lead.

At this stage in my career, my greatest challenges have been to develop skills to navigate through this "imposter syndrome" in order to be a leader, to understand and communicate both the library and IT perspectives, and to act in the interest of all when necessary. Despite my positive experiences and mostly equitable foundation, it hasn't always been easy being a woman in the technology field, though tempered within libraries[6]. Here are three things I've learned along the way.

1. Accept That You May Not Know Everything, but Strive to Still Learn More

My career hasn't been without doubt or insecurities along the way. When asked a question that I do not know the answer to, in that quiet space between question and answer, I worry that I'll be seen as a fraud. It's been useful to learn that I'm not alone in this thinking though it doesn't excuse it. I have had to be willing to say, "I don't know" or some variation of, "I'd like to give your question further thought; may I get back to you?" bell hooks writes, "Academics fear confessing that we do not have the 'answer' because we are afraid that audiences will shame us, or worse, see us as not very smart. When one adds race, gender

5 Valerie Young, *The Secret Thoughts of Successful Women: Why Capable People Suffer from the Impostor Syndrome and How to Thrive in Spite of It* (New York: Crown Business, 2011).

6 Erin Marie Golub, "Gender Divide in Librarianship: Past, Present and Future." *Library Student Journal* 5 (2010).

and class into the equation, it becomes all the more risky to be perceived as not worthy, not good."[7]

I don't have a computer science degree, but I manage those who do; and I occasionally worry that I won't be respected because of a perceived lack of understanding or experience. I'm often the only woman in the room, and there's always the thought that I'll be seen as lesser or talked over. I am not the first woman to feel her confidence waver when others seem to understand the concepts more deeply[8]. Regardless of this fear, my experience has taught me that it's important to be honest with myself, my team, and others when I don't understand something.

I once worked alongside a supervisor who used all the right buzzwords, but never seemed to fundamentally understand what she was talking about. I watched as the team under her lost respect for her, the project failed as a result, and ultimately she moved on. Since becoming the head of my team, I make an effort to let my team know that sometimes I don't have the answer–or that they may know better than I. I have confidence in my team, and it's important to me that they know that I trust them and value their knowledge. As the only woman on the team, and as the supervisor, I know that I am working against gender constructs. I also know that I may be representing women. If I don't understand something, it does a disservice to myself and my team by not owning up to it.

2. Learn From Failure and Successes Alike

My colleagues reached out to me to see if I would build a website that would meet their needs. When I had a working prototype, it became clear to all of us that although I had created what had been asked of me, it was not a good solution for the

---

7   bell hooks, *Teaching Critical Thinking : Practical Wisdom* (New York: Routledge, 2010), 67.

8   Margolis and Fisher, *Unlocking the Clubhouse*, 77, 82-83.

project despite meeting the original request. I also knew that a member of my staff would have the time and was better suited skill-wise to work on the project. In that moment, I learned what all supervisors need to learn to do: to step back, delegate, and allow their staff to be able to make decisions with authority. It was ok to fail in that instance and to recognize that meeting the goals of the project and of the institution held precedence over my own ego. I met with my colleagues and I told them, "I know this is what you asked for, but it's not meeting your needs. I know someone who will do a better job by building from the ground-up. I'm going to clear their schedule so they can give it the attention the project deserves." Ultimately as the head of my team, the accountability lay with me and to ensure that the project succeeded, that meant putting the right person for the job in the right spot.

3. Push Against the Dominant Culture When Appropriate

"...there are situations where in order to be heard you have to forgo the usual rules, starting with the belief that you always have to follow the rules."

Valerie Young[9]

To interrupt someone while they are speaking is often seen as a breach of conversational rules. However, interrupting someone isn't necessarily a negative. Sometimes we interrupt to show enthusiasm or that we are listening. Alternatively, interrupting may be utilized to gain control or power over the conversation. Who you are, regarding status and gender, and how you inter-

---

9   Young, *The Secret Thoughts of Successful Women*, 116.

rupt can work for or against you[10]. For example, when the person doing the talking is a VIP, they're often given more leeway. This can make sense to some degree, but when that person's actions come at the expense of other people, it's less acceptable. In moments like that, I believe it's time to break the rules.

Once, during a joint library / IT meeting, forty-five minutes into the hour-long meeting, the same man was speaking. When I glanced over at my supervisor, I could see his brow knit and furrow as if he too were internally struggling with how to politely deal with this top-level IT member who had co-opted our meeting with an unrequested soliloquy. Dialogue is important, but it can't happen if the players do not respect each other's time. Looking to the project manager I thought, "Surely she will rope him back in, and bring us back on target to the matter at hand," but she remained silent. For women, there is a fine line in how and when one speaks up[11] without jeopardizing one's career. It was in that moment, that I realized two things: I wasn't alone with being uncomfortable with him speaking for so long out of turn, and also that no one was comfortable with interrupting him. For me this realization in the meeting meant speaking up: "I'd like to thank you for your comments, and bring us back to the matter at hand." I interrupted, and in doing so, opened up the floor for more voices to speak.

By monopolizing the conversation, this man was silencing the rest of us in the room[12]. I can't say for certain that gender was at the center of it, but I do think it warrants acknowledging that gender stereotypes of passivity exist. Women who are

10   Deborah James and Sandra Clarke, "Chapter 9. Women, Men, and Interruptions: A Critical Review," in *Gender and Conversational Interaction*. Ed. Deborah Tannen, (Oxford University Press, 1993), 231-280.

11   Sheryl Sandberg, and Adam Grant, "Speaking While Female," *The New York Times,* January 12, 2015, accessed 03/12/2017, https://www.nytimes.com/2015/01/11/opinion/sunday/speaking-while-female.html.

12   hooks, *Teaching Critical Thinking*, 73.

taught to be quiet, polite, and accepting may tread lightly in an effort to not be penalized for being anything but feminine. In my career, as in the earlier example, I have had to teach myself to speak up. My role at the library is to provide a connection between the library and IT. If the library was effectively being silenced or derailed by IT, it is my role to restore the situation so that communication between both entities reopens.

Final Comments

Within the library, I am respected and sought out for technical help and expertise. The library is separate from the main campus' IT department, and manages its own IT team. This affords the library some leeway in developing our own projects, but also makes us a drop in the campus-wide bucket simply due to the size of the university. I've had to speak up to be noticed so that the library and my team are able to do their jobs. I have learned to step outside of my own comfort and voice concerns, ideas, and even doubts to those above me. My experience taken individually is an anecdote, but combined with others, can provide a more comprehensive view of how gender, technology, and libraries are, and continue to be, intertwined.

From Imposter to Contender: The Women of Library IT

Christina Mune

#ChangeAgent #Advice #DefyingStereotypes
#EverydaySexism #ImposterSyndrome

The feminization of library science as a profession is well known. Every stereotype of a librarian starts with a woman. While undeniably problematic in a sociological sense, for me, the feminization of librarianship made the profession more attractive. As a young person deciding on my master's degree program the thought of working for, with, and eventually managing well-read educated women with a penchant for public service was both exciting and comforting. In my inexperience, I imagined there would be no glass ceiling to break, no workplace gender discrimination to navigate, no barriers to the top positions I knew I wanted. Of course, after getting my first library job I realized how incredibly naive that was, but still, I enjoy working for organizations with female representation from top to bottom.

It's also been my experience that in libraries, a little technological know-how and a willingness to learn can quickly propel you into an exciting technology role, regardless of gender. For a profession that increasingly relies on technology to deliver core services there is a critical shortage of applicable skills within the profession. This can be attributed to a rapid paradigm shift in the delivery of library services from physical to digital that has left mid-career professionals ill prepared for emerging library positions. It is also an artifact of LIS students' lingering misconception that their education should prepare them to become literature-loving bibliophiles that spend their days rooting through rare book stacks. For the profession, this is a problem. For the tech-loving MLIS holding woman, this is an amazing opportunity.

While reference, technical services, and public service leads and department managers are often firmly entrenched in their positions with multiple potential successors already in line, newly formed technology positions may be up for grabs by those willing to take on the responsibilities and risks. These positions sometimes come with more decision-making power and budget influence than traditional roles, which also means a high profile and even higher expectations. Library administrators must recognize technological prowess and propensity early on and reward it accordingly to fill the required technology positions. For those of us willing to accept the challenge, exhibiting these skills can equal a professional slingshot. My own trajectory from Online Learning Librarian to Digital Initiatives Coordinator to IT Manager in the first six years of my career provides an excellent example.

However, even with these opportunities in play, the fact remains that men disproportionately hold library and technology leadership positions in comparison to their representation within the profession. ARL's 2014-2015 salary survey found that while men made up approximately 38 percent of library staff they accounted for 67.5 percent of library technology department heads and 42 percent of library directorships.[13] In the large state university system where I'm an IT director of one of the larger university libraries, thirteen out of twenty-three (56.5 percent) library deans are male. Four out of five individuals responsible for digital library services and content employed by our chancellor's office are men. A 2017 review of library staff directories for my system found that of the eighteen campuses where a director, manager or coordinator of technology or IT could be easily identified, thirteen were male (72 percent). Even in this overwhelmingly female profession with plenty of technology roles available for women, we still find ourselves frequently reporting to male managers because of the inequitable distribution of leadership roles. So while there seems to be plenty of room for women in library IT, these statistics show significant barriers must still be overcome on our way to the top. And at the top, we're likely to look around and see a lot more male faces than we're used to in our profession.

Whether a woman in library IT is traditionally trained in her technology role or inhabiting it from the pathway of digital librarianship, emerging technologies, or technical services she is likely struggling against not only gender equity issues as an IT person, but also against library and/or librarian stereotypes. I've heard countless IT professionals express surprise that the library has or needs an IT department: "Don't you just check out books over there?" Asking them to consider a woman who was recently a librarian or library staff as their technical equal seems a daunting if not impossible task. Especially when that woman might be feeling, as I frequently do, like an imposter.

Imposter phenomenon has been described as: "an internal experience of intellectual phoniness that appears to

---

13   "ARL Annual Salary Survey 2014-2015," *Association of Research Libraries*, (Washington DC: Association of Research Libraries, 2015), 18-19, accessed July 27, 2017, http://publications.arl.org/ARL-Annual-Salary-Survey-2014-2015/.

be particularly prevalent and intense among a select sample of high achieving women... despite outstanding academic and professional accomplishments, women who experience the impostor phenomenon persist in believing that they are really not bright and have fooled anyone who thinks otherwise."[14]

I reluctantly admit that I cried my first time reading this description because it so succinctly described my greatest secret fear–that I am a total fraud as a library IT director. I'm not a network engineer, I can't write amazing python scripts, and I've never configured an LDAP server. These are the things I ask the people that work for me to do. So what that I've taught myself CSS and JavaScript from online tutorials, built a media server out of a Raspberry Pi, and implemented a new discovery system for a consortium of twenty-three libraries? I'm not one of the guys. I don't have a computer science or IT degree. I don't really belong here. Every time I'm on a technical committee or task force and get asked to make an agenda, take the minutes, or schedule the next meeting while my male counterparts aren't requested to do those clerical-like tasks, those feelings of fraudulence are reinforced.

So what can we do when we feel like an imposter and are treated like an imposter even while experiencing great career success? How can we overcome this imposter phenomenon?

I recommend two things:

---

14   Pauline R. Clance and Suzanne A. Imes, "The Imposter Phenomenon in High Achieving Women: Dynamics and Therapeutic Intervention," *Psychotherapy: Theory, Research and Practice* 15, no. 3 (1978): 241 quoted in Sonja Rohrmann, Myriam N. Bechtoldt and Mona Leonhardt, "Validation of the Impostor Phenomenon among Managers," *Frontiers in Psychology* 7 (June 2016), Introduction, accessed July 27, 2017 http://journal.frontiersin. org/article/10.3389/fpsyg.2016.00821/full.

First, watch Amy Cuddy's 2012 TED Talk, "Your Body Language May Shape Who You Are."[15] Cuddy's message to not fake it 'til you make it but instead to "fake it 'til you become it" has been critical to my success. Taking up lots of space in the meeting room, proclaiming mastery over topics and projects, speaking up when it seems like a risk, thinking I'm smarter than a CIO (or at least as important as one)–these behaviors have actually helped me convince myself that I can do this. That I can be this. I promise, that confidence is infectious.

Second, change the language. Replace the term imposter with contender, in our minds and in our speech. Rather than feeling duplicitous, library IT women should adopt labels like defier, darer, and dynamo when describing themselves and their qualities. We are trailblazers, pathfinders, and up-starts. In a society that reveres start-ups and innovation, IT women should be lauded as career-hacking entrepreneurs.

Library IT women need to acknowledge that for some of us, our way to the IT world might be different, but still valuable. Our experience, hard work, and capacity are unique and priceless not bogus or fraudulent. Our gender and our training make us invaluably unique, not a liability. In a profession in which lifelong learning is an ethos, why should we ever consider ourselves imposters? We're just always in that process of becoming. Becoming something new, something more, something powerful. I challenge the women of library IT to demand that they be seen as I see them – daring trailblazers applying their ever-growing skills to defying ridiculous stereotypes and misconceptions. I ask them to see other IT women that way, to share these new terms with them,

---

15   Amy Cuddy, "Your Body Language May Shape Who You Are," June 2012, TED video, 20:56, https://www.ted.com/talks/amy_cuddy_your_body_language_shapes_who_you_are.

to lift them up. I wouldn't be in a position to write this essay today if it weren't for female colleagues that lifted me in the wake of their own rise. I challenge too library deans and directors, IT managers, and IT professionals to blow up their own preconceptions and instead value the diversity of experience, education, and perspective library IT women bring to the table. And please don't ask us to take the meeting minutes (unless our male counterparts are asked to do the same).

GratITude

Leah M Root

#ChangeAgents #Influencers #Mentorship #RoleModels

This is a list of kudos and thank you to the people, places, things, and media, that influenced and encouraged me to follow and stay on the path as a woman in IT.

I believe this list truly shows how I came to be.

My mom: For buying an Atari 400 because her "town rival" had a Commodore 64; I became good at Space Invaders, Missile Command, and Star Raiders. I also learned how to create some wild graphic animations with BASIC.

My 5th grade teacher, Mr. Watson (circa 1981): For teaching us BASIC programming using his TRS-80, and recognizing that some of us had aptitude for math, science, and logic, but did not necessarily learn those subjects via traditional teaching methods.

Carl Sagan's COSMOS, Disney's TRON, Star Wars, Battlestar Galactica, Bionic Woman, Wonder Woman, Star Trek, Space 1999, and Doctor Who: Maybe there was misogyny and sexism in those shows and movies, but all I saw as a young child and pre-teen at that time were these things: amazing worlds and dimensions, science, technology, and women who could kick butt despite obstacles. (There were some creepy monsters in some of those shows, but I still wanted to watch them, even if I was hiding behind the couch.)

My high school art teacher and literary magazine advisors, Emily Aumiller (RIP) and Gail Rhinelander: They saw potential in me that I did not see. They saw that I could draw, write, put together things, match patterns, and make things work.

My technical drawing and AutoCAD teacher, Mr. Davies: He did not care that I was female, or that I struggled in math – he just wanted precise illustrations, and the ability to see something in "all dimensions."

My biology teacher, Mr. Burr (RIP): For recognizing my ability to match patterns, to illustrate cellular, anatomical, genetic, and physical concepts, and basically take his classes seriously.

My friend, Gretchen: For convincing me to apply for the imaging arts master's degree program at Rochester Institute of Technology (RIT) (which is now a dozen different branches of computer animation, game design, rendering, graphics, and programming).

My RIT professors, Marla Schweppe and Erik Timmerman (RIP): They emphasized analysis and pattern matching, whether it was in cinematography, scenery, movie plots, walk cycles, film and video editing, 3-D lighting, or programming. Once again, I saw the same patterns in Actionscript, Lingo, Visual Basic, C++, and Hypercard, that I saw many years prior in my exposure to BASIC.

My brother, Martin H. Bosworth (RIP 1975-2010): My brother was an advocate for Net Neutrality, Consumer rights, Electronic privacy rights, Human rights, Creative Commons, and Open Access. He was a prolific writer. His work still lives on the Internet. I hope his legacy and wisdom lives on in me, and within those whose lives he touched.

Cats and dogs I've had throughout my life: They did not judge me. They were always there for me whether I was happy, distraught, angry, successful, or starving.

Me, myself, and I: For the drive to learn what I needed to learn, despite any limitations, hostility, assumptions, excuses, threats, drama, harassment, or other boundaries that got in my way–in order to survive, make a living, and become a respected woman in the world of IT.

What a Difference a Decade (or Three) Makes

Kathy Watts

#ChangeAgent #CSEducation #Generations #GirlsInIT
#RoleModels #SelfConfidence #VisionForFutureForWomen

When I was a child, my two favorite toys were my Lego police station and my Matchbox car city. I also had a Barbie Fashion Face and a Baby Alive. In the early 1970s, it was not typical for parents to buy what were considered boys' toys for their daughters. Thankfully, my parents let me follow all of my interests when purchasing toys for me. My parents' gender-neutral toy purchasing taught me that my interests, rather than my gender identity, determined my play and my hobbies. That lesson extended to my career choice, and was further reinforced by stories of my grandmother selling lawnmowers to golf courses in the 1920s. The lesson there was that no interest was off-limits for a potential career. Despite these early lessons and my dabbling in code in my teens (mainly by reading how-to articles in my father's computer magazines), I did not initially pursue computer science or technology as a career. My high school experience with technology was more stereotypical. Personal computers were very new then, but my high school did have one small Apple II lab. The one time I went in, it was filled with boys and did not seem like a place for me. I can hardly blame the boys for my feeling excluded. They didn't even notice I was there, as they were so absorbed by their activities on the computers. No one excluded me. I excluded myself.

Unfortunately, my reaction to the computer lab full of boys is not unique. It is one example of a lack of self-efficacy: a doubt as to my ability to participate, to learn, and to succeed. It is a self-perpetuating process that has been made into a theory, applied to career choices, and backed up by research. Nancy Heilbronner in particular, has studied how women choose to enter STEM fields. She identified four factors that influence career choices for men and women: ability, interest, self-efficacy, and educational experiences[16]. She concluded that "Belief in their own ability to do well in STEM appeared to be a significant factor in determining whether individuals stayed in STEM."[17] Like many other women, despite the lack of explicit statements otherwise, when I peered into that Apple II lab, I didn't believe I belonged there.

Thirty years later, I observed a similar situation with another high school girl, my daughter. Like me at the same age, she has an interest in computers and programming. Also like me, she has an ability in programming many of her peers do not. Her educational experiences, however, are markedly different. Multiple computer science courses are offered at her high school, including AP Computer Science. Unfortunately, one thing remains disturbingly similar. My daughter's first high school computer science class was mostly boys, a phenomenon repeated across the United States. In 2016, only 23% of students taking an AP Computer Science course were female.[18] For some stu-

---

16   Nancy N. Heilbronner, "Stepping Onto the STEM Pathway: Factors Affecting Talented Students' Declaration of STEM Majors in College," *Journal for the Education of the Gifted* 34, no 6 (2011).

17   Ibid., 896.

18   College Board, *Program Summary Report* 2016.

dents, the opportunity to take computer science doesn't even exist. In 2016, 22% of high school principals reported that no computer science courses were offered at their school.[19]

At this point, my experience and my daughter's diverge. She has chosen to major in computer science in college. The key differences between our experiences are modeling and affirmation. She personally knows women employed in IT, female programmers, and women pursuing advanced degrees in computer engineering. She has been encouraged and supported by both her parents and her teachers to pursue computer science. She has been told it is for her, that she is good at it, and that her interest can be turned into a career. Particularly important for her was receiving recognition, an outstanding achievement award, from her freshman computer science teacher. Albert Bandura's original research on self-efficacy would say that those role models and affirmations taught my daughter that she has the ability to work and succeed in computer science[20], and Heilbronner would argue that mindset is essential for anyone – male or female – to choose and persist in a STEM field.[21]

Achievement, persistence, and success in technology fields are determined by other factors in addition to ability and interest. Separated by thirty years, my daughter and I both stood at the computer lab door and peered in. My daughter went in because she was invited in, made welcome, and affirmed. I went in twenty years later. The difference was a sense of belonging. My experience of self-doubt in the boy-dominated Apple II lab was a key one for me. I didn't pursue computer science as an undergraduate, not because anyone told me it wasn't for me; rather, because no one told me it was for me. Ceasing the nega-

---

19   Google Inc., and Gallup Inc., *Trends in the State of Computer Science in U.S. K-12 Schools*, 10.

20   Albert Bandura, "Self-efficacy: Toward a Unifying Theory of Behavioral Change," *Psychological Review* 84 (1977), 197-198.

21   Heilbronner, "Stepping Onto the STEM Pathway," 893.

tive attitude – "girls can't do math and science" – is a necessary first step to getting more women into IT. The next necessary step is to voice the positive – girls and women succeed, achieve, and enjoy math, science, and technology. The self-perpetuating self-efficacy cycle can become a positive one through role models, affirmation, and belonging. Girls and women today should all receive the lessons I learned early on: that Legos and Matchbox cars are for girls, that interest drives play, hobbies, and careers, and that they belong in the computer lab.

TELL IMPOSTER SYNDROME TO TAKE A SEAT

Kathy Zadrozny

#ChangeAgent #AddWomen #ImposterSyndrome #PublicSpeaking

I am not a fan of public speaking. I clench my jaw, my face gets red, and every so often I even get hives. Yet ever since I've entered the library tech world, I've presented at about three conferences each year. Why would I do this to myself? Sure, there are always a few people who come up to me afterward and tell me how they never knew about XYZ and now want to do more with it, or how they can apply what they learned at work tomorrow. It is always great to get that feedback when you share with peers. But let's be selfish for a minute and ask, what do I get out of it?

I do not consider myself an expert in anything. I am always learning. Our industry is always changing, and the lines that draw borders around what is considered "our industry" blur and flex constantly. So when a coworker asked me to present with him at a conference in another state, my first thought was, "Why me? I'm no expert in this." This is when I point out the statistic that women generally feel like they are not experts in their trade, even when they are highly capable.[22] Also, that men have the self-confidence to apply for the job they don't have all the requirements for, or apply to the conference when they still aren't sure what the heck they are going to talk about.[23] We need to give ourselves that same confidence as a white man in tech. That being said, when I said "sure" to doing the presentation, it wasn't because I overcame my lack of confidence and all of a sudden felt like an expert. I thought there was no chance our presentation proposal would get accepted, so I obviously had nothing to worry about. I would not be found out as a fraud, as I so obviously am, or for not being an expert in All The Things, because there was no chance our proposal would make it in.

Our presentation proposal got accepted. Cue hyperventilating and self-doubt.

In putting together the presentation, I had to articulate how to do processes I do often with little thought. How does one break down and explain a daily task, like turning a brainstorming session into a project spec sheet? The analyzation needed to turn those mechanisms into a presentation made me consider my process, reshape the procedures of that task, and actually made me create a better workflow. Additionally, I realized that I was actually more of an expert in the topic than I realized. Creating a presentation with a coworker gave me a better working relationship with him, which led to more interesting projects at work, since he knew I could aid him with specific problems. That presentation sparked the idea for another presentation, because I asked myself, "what if I take this one bit and transform it?" This leads to a chain reaction of curiosi-

---

22   Pauline R. Clance and Suzanne A. Imes, "The Imposter Phenomenon in High Achieving Women: Dynamics and Therapeutic Intervention," *Psychotherapy: Theory, Research and Practice* 15, no. 3 (1978): 242.

23   Katty Kay and Claire Shipman, "The Confidence Gap," *The Atlantic*, May 2014, https://www.theatlantic.com/magazine/archive/2014/05/the-confidence-gap/359815/

ty in areas that you want to explore and share with your peers. This is why I stand in front of strangers talking about things I don't consider myself an expert in. This is why you should take a chance and do so too.

It is so easy to say "I'm not an expert in that" and decide never to share your experiences or lessons in an open forum. None of us are experts. So, if you know just a little bit about something, share it. There is likely someone who has been curious about it or gets turned on to this new-to-them thing, all because you put yourself out there. Share your knowledge and see where your curiosity leads you. Push past the fear and take "the big step" that is right for you. Start small, with a lightning talk or a workshop for your fellow staff members, but put yourself out there. Take a chance, and you'll be surprised at what will blossom from that one step.

Editors

Jenny Brandon earned a BA in interdisciplinary humanities at Michigan State University, and an MLIS from Wayne State University. She is a self-taught web designer/front end developer, and is currently employed in Web Services at Michigan State University. She is also a reference librarian. She previously wrote a book chapter, "Librarians as Web Designers, in Envisioning Our Preferred Future: New Services, Jobs and Directions," by Bradford Lee Eden.

Sharon Ladenson is Gender and Communication Studies Librarian at Michigan State University. Her writing on feminist pedagogy and critical information literacy is included in works such as *Critical Library Instruction: Theories and Methods* (from Library Juice Press) and *Critical Library Pedagogy Handbook* (from the Association of College and Research Libraries). She is an active member of the Women and Gender Studies Section (WGSS) of the Association of College and Research Libraries, and has presented with WGSS colleagues at the National Women's Studies Association Annual Conference.

Kelly Sattler has a Bachelor of Science degree in computer engineering and spent 12 years in corporate IT before earning her MLIS degree from University of Illinois-Urbana/Champaign. Currently, she is the Head of Web Services at Michigan State University Libraries. She is an active member in ALA's Library Information and Technology Association (LITA) and ALA's Biblioquilters.

Contributors

Cathleen Carstens has been the Internet/Technology Librarian at a public library in the Rochester, New York area since January 3, 2000. She enjoys challenges and also appreciates always having something new to learn. The best thing for her about working in technology in a public library is having a direct positive impact on peoples' lives. She loves seeing a person's face light up with happiness when they are finally successful at using the computer.

Tara Coleman is the Web Services Librarian for Kansas State University Libraries in Manhattan, Kansas. She is responsible for the oversight of a well-managed web presence for the libraries. She is the lead in design, usability, content, and function of the website. She holds degrees in English and Library and Information Studies.

Suzanna Conrad obtained her MSLIS from the University of Illinois, Urbana-Champaign in 2011 and her MBA from the University of East London in 2006. As Head of Library Information Systems at California State University, Sacramento, Suzanna provides leadership on the development and articulation of vision, strategic directions, and priorities for library information technology. Suzanna's research interests include human-computer interaction, scholarly communication, and ethics in librarianship.

Susie Speer Corbett has an MSLS from UNC–Chapel Hill. She is currently the Vice President of Life Science Intelligence at the North Carolina Biotechnology Center, leading her teams in their efforts to provide top-notch information tools, technologies and infrastructure for the Center and its work to support the life sciences industry. Throughout her career, Susie has managed IT teams, merging the technical and theoretical best practices for information and knowledge management.

Jenelys Cox is currently an Institutional Repository Manager and Application Support Technician at the University of Denver's University Libraries. She has a Master of Library and Information Science from the University of Denver and a B.S. in Mathematics and Computer Science from the University of Colorado, Colorado Springs.

Janet Crum received her MLS from the University of Washington in 1992. Since then, she has held positions in library technology and administration in academic and medical libraries in four states and three time zones. She is currently Head, Library Technology Services at Northern Arizona University in Flagstaff, AZ. In her off hours, Janet attempts to make plants grow in a volcano field at 7000 feet elevation, an effort for which—much like a career in library technology—stubbornness is a virtue.

Allison Deluca is a Web Services Librarian II at Nova Southeastern University. She is passionate about user-centered web development for libraries. Her interest in web development began at the age of 15 and has only continued to grow ever since. Prior to this position she worked as a Systems Librarian, and before that as a Medical Librarian at Florida Atlantic University.

Kate Dohe is the Digital Programs and Initiatives Manager at the University of Maryland Libraries. Prior to joining UMD, she was the Digital Services Librarian at Georgetown University, and the digital librarian for an academic textbook publisher in California. She earned her MLISc. from the University of Hawai'i, and also holds a BSEd. in Speech and Theater from Missouri State University.

Marcia L. Dority Baker is an Assistant Director, Academic Technologies with the Office of Information Technology (ITS) at the University of Nebraska-Lincoln. Prior to joining ITS, Marcia was an Associate Professor of Law Library and Access Services Librarian, at Schmid Law Library, University of Nebraska College of Law.

Olufunmilayo Fati holds Master of Library and Information Studies and B-Tech in Computer Science. She is currently a Systems Librarian with the University of Jos Library in Nigeria where she has worked as a Systems Programmer/Librarian for over nine years. Her research interests include digital libraries, digitalization of work processes, discovery systems and services, and evaluation of integrated library systems.

Kevin Finkenbinder, Web Developer for the MSU Libraries, started programming Apple II computers in 1978 and has been an IT professional since 1994. His career includes programming, systems administration, technical training, database and telecom experience. Kevin earned a BS in Computer Science from the University of Colorado and an MDiv from Midwestern Baptist Theological Seminary. Kevin and his wife Amy want to see their daughter and two sons succeed in ways they never imagined.

Deloris Jackson Foxworth is pursuing a graduate certificate in career services at Western Kentucky University (WKU) and works full-time as an academic advisor at the University of Kentucky (UK). Previously she was a lecturer in the School of Information Science at UK and prior to that served 2 years as technology manager at the Scott County Public Library. She has master's degrees in library science and communication. She lives with her husband and two daughters.

Alexandra Gallin-Parisi is an Instruction Librarian and Assistant Professor at Trinity University in San Antonio, Texas. Her research focuses broadly on inclusion and equity, and she publishes about motherhood, disability, academic success, and unheard voices in the academic library. Alex is the liaison to five social science departments, serves as an academic advisor to first-year students, and teaches a credit-bearing academic success course for student-athletes.

Denise Garofalo has worked with technology in public, school, special, and academic libraries in New England and New York State. She has presented at various national and regional conferences, written chapters and articles, and taught technology-related courses as an adjunct at the Department of Information Science at the University at Albany. Her hobbies include hiking, gardening, science fiction, and video games.

Lynne Grigsby has worked as a programmer and project manager in libraries for over 30 years and is currently the Head of Library IT at the University of California, Berkeley.

Julie Guzzetta works as an information technology consultant at Portland State University, in the great Pacific Northwest. In her spare time, she enjoys drinking a good cup of coffee, studying math, hiking, reading, and playing chess (not necessarily in that order). It is her dream to visit Italy one day.

Kat Hagedorn is the Head of Digital Content & Collections at the University of Michigan Library. She is responsible for facilitating creation and maintenance of user-centered, curated, preserved digital collections and digital content services, as well as programmatic involvement in building and scaling the division's digital content and collections platform. Kat received her Master's in Information from the University of Michigan, and has worked at the U-M Library for over 15 years.

Robin Hastings is the Library Services Consultant for the Northeast Kansas Library System (NEKLS). In that capacity, she provides technology and consulting on library services to 40+ libraries in the NEKLS region. She has presented all over the world on Cloud Computing, Project Management, Disaster Planning and many other topics. Robin is the author of 4 books on library-related topics as well as several articles in library-related journals.

Dana Haugh is the Web Services Librarian at Stony Brook University Libraries where she leads the design and development of the library's web presences. Her research interests include web design & development, marketing & outreach in libraries, open access, and information literacy. She received her MLS from Queens College and BA in English from Stony Brook University.

Margaret Heller has been Digital Services Librarian at Loyola University Chicago since 2014; prior to that she was Web Services Librarian at Dominican University. She is on the board of LITA, the Library Information Technology Division of the American Library Association. She is a member of the Code4Lib community and has organized national and local conferences for that group. She was on the founding board in 2009 of the Read/Write Library Chicago.

Amy Hezel is an ILS & E-Resource librarian and assistant professor at Regis University in Denver, CO. She has worked in the library software industry and in many different types of libraries, including museum, digital archive, public, and academic libraries. Her research interests include library history, the history of the book and printing, and 20th century American literature.

Donna Kaminski is the Technical Support Coordinator at Coates Library at Trinity University in San Antonio, Texas.

Tari Keller attended Miami University (in Ohio) where she earned a bachelor of arts in mathematics and a master of education in educational media. After five years of teaching junior high mathematics, she earned her master of library science from Indiana University (in Indiana). Her first professional library job was as a cataloger at the University of Kentucky. She stayed to become their first systems librarian and loved every minute of it!

Karen C. Knox is the Director of the Orion Township Public Library in Lake Orion, Michigan. She has worked professionally in libraries for 17 years after earning her Masters in Library and Information Science from the University of Texas at Austin in 2000. She has a Bachelor of Science in Computer Science from the University of Michigan. She has presented and published over the years, as she enjoys sharing her experiences with others.

Vincci Kwong is currently the Head of Library Web Services at the Franklin D. Schurz Library, IU South Bend, where she provides leadership and direction for the library website. Projects she participates in include responsive web design, web content management, usability studies, mobile applications and authentication. Other than emerging technologies, Vincci is also interested in leadership and administration.

Catherine Larson leads Systems & Technology at the NYU Health Sciences Library. She holds an MS in Library and Information Science from the University of Illinois Urbana-Champaign and a BFA in Art and Technology from the School of the Art Institute of Chicago. Prior to working in libraries, Catherine worked in the private sector designing and building websites for small businesses to Fortune 500s.

Hong Ma manages and provides leadership for the Library Systems Department, which is responsible for maintenance and development of information technology infrastructure, productions, and services across the University Libraries at Loyola University Chicago. Prior to Loyola, she was Information Systems Librarian for the University of Miami libraries. She has been actively involved with library technology community such as LITA. She writes and presents nationally.

Amanda Hartman McLellan is the Head of Applications and Digital Services at East Carolina University, and Adjunct Lecturer at the University of Illinois School of Information Sciences. Her research interests include library technology, usability and user experience, and library management. A member of Rotary International, Amanda enjoys giving back to the community, baking, and spending time with her husband, dog, and cats.

Christina Mune, MLIS is a librarian, a feminist and the IT Director at San Jose State University Library. She often writes about library technology and occasionally about women in American history. At work Christina's interested in digital scholarship, IoT and destroying impostor syndrome. At home she's interested in astronomy, reading sci-fi and cats.

Este Paskausky Pope is Head of Digital Programs in Frost Library at Amherst College. Prior work experiences include supporting production library systems at Yale University, implementing the Canvas learning management system at Coconino Community College, building the digital scholarship program at the Boston College Libraries, and coordinating the library renovation and website redesign at Wentworth Institute of Technology. Este is also a writer, a hiker, a yogi, a knitter, a mother, a spouse.

Leah M. Root is a web developer for Milne Library at the State University of New York at Geneseo. She has been around the intertubes since the days of NetScape and Mosaic. Growing up during the 1980s (age of TRON), she was raised "command line" and learned BASIC programming on an Atari 400, graduating to a TRS-80. Leah now codes in C#/, PHP, SQL, Javascript, and works in several different platforms and operating systems. When not tethered to a computer or mobile device, Leah hikes with her dogs, transports rescue animals, and trains in archery and martial arts.

Jeff Rynhart is a software engineer and developer who specializes in the design and implementation of web-based computer systems, working with both client and server side applications. His experience ranges from creating data processing algorithms to graphic design. Jeff began his education in electronics engineering, but moved on to computer science after completing his degree. He worked as a C++ developer before starting his current position as Systems Programmer at the University of Denver.

Rhela Sudo Pseudonym for author who wants to remain anonymous.

Alisha Taylor received her MLS from Emporia State University and has a postgraduate certificate in Education from Greenwich University and Bachelor of Science degree in Chemistry from London Metropolitan University. Alisha currently, since November 2017, serves as the Monographic & Media Cataloging Coordinator in Content Access Management (CAM) at the University of Illinois at Urbana-Champaign Library. A few places she has previously worked are Portland State University Library, Ingram Book Company, and Backstage Library Works.

Rachel Vacek is the Head of Design & Discovery, a department providing front-end web development, design, content strategy, user research, accessibility expertise, and UX strategy across the University of Michigan Library web presence. Rachel regularly teaches workshops and gives presentations at local and national library conferences on UX, library web technologies, and library leadership. She is a past ALA Emerging Leader, a Library Journal Mover & Shaker, former LITA President, and a Leading Change Institute alumna.

Stephanie Walker is the Dean of Libraries & Information Resources at the University of North Dakota. Previously, she served as Chief Librarian & Executive Director of Academic Information Technologies at Brooklyn College. She has also served in managerial, library IT, or IT liaison roles at Harvard University's Countway Library, Mount Saint Vincent University (Canada), and the University of Toronto, and has held IT positions in programming, technical support, and database administration.

Kathy A. Watts is the Access Services Librarian at Whitworth University in Spokane, Washington. She holds an MLIS and an M.Ed. in Educational Technology. Her first programming experience was tinkering with BASIC on a TI-99/4A home computer in the early 1980s. Since then, her work at a software company and in academic libraries has afforded her many opportunities to get lost in the puzzle-solving nature of programming. And she still plays with Legos.

Sharon Whitfield is an Emerging Technologies Librarian at Cooper Medical School of Rowan University. Since entering librarianship, Whitfield has always worked within library technology department. Whitfield enjoys programming and bringing new technologies to life. Whitfield is currently pursuing her doctorate in educational leadership from Rowan University. Her dissertation topic focuses on gender and organizational citizenship behaviors in library technology departments.

Melissa Wisner is a Project Manager and IT Administrator currently working at Yale University. Her education is in the intersection of humanities and technology administration, and library science. Her professional interests include how libraries' relationship with IT and technology could be improved, and using analytics to make decisions about service, strategy, and space. She believes libraries should borrow more from business models in other industries, while still upholding libraries' core values of knowledge, dissemination, and accessibility.

Jingjing Wu is the Web assistant librarian in the Texas Tech University Libraries. She earned her Master of Science in Library and Information Science from Wayne State University and Bachelor of Engineering in Optical Instrumentation with a minor in Information Science from Zhejiang University. Her research interests include Web technologies, user experience in libraries, data processing and analysis, and library research methods.

Shea-Tinn (Sheila) Yeh is a Ph.D. candidate in Computer Science and Information Systems at the University of Colorado Denver Business School. She has also earned a M.L.S. degree in Library and Information Science from the University of Maryland and a M.S.E. degree in Industrial and Human Computer Engineering from Wright State University. Sheila is currently the Assistant University Librarian for Library Information Technology at the University of Hawai'i at Mānoa.

Becky Yoose is the Library Applications and Systems Manager at the Seattle Public Library. Her work and interests fall into the many intersections of technology and libraries from the practicalities of adoption or non-adoption of technologies in libraries to the way technology has changed the culture of modern librarianship. Her library community work includes code4lib, LibTechWomen, Mashcat, and Troublesome Catalogers and Magical Metadata Fairies, as well as connecting other communities, such as Write The Docs, to the library world.

Kathy Zadrozny is a Web Developer and Graphic Design Specialist at the University of Chicago Library. She began her design career in advertising and quickly became interested in all things code. Kathy spends most of her time on front-end development, UI design, and taste-testing whisky. She also co-founded the Letter Writers Alliance, which is a worldwide organization dedicated to preserving the art of letter writing.

Bibliography

Abbate, Janet. *Recoding Gender: Women's Changing Participation in Computing*. Cambridge, MA: MIT Press, 2012.

Allen, David. *Getting Things Done: The Art of Stress-Free Productivity*. New York: Penguin Books, 2015.

Ashcraft, Catherine, Brad McLain, and Elizabeth Eger. "Women in Tech: The Facts," 2016. https://www.ncwit.org/sites/default/files/resources/ncwit_women-in-it_2016-full-report_final-web06012016.pdf.

Aspray, William. *Women and Underrepresented Minorities in Computing*. History of Computing. Switzerland: Springer International Publishing, 2016.

Bandura, Albert. "Self-Efficacy: Toward a Unifying Theory of Behavioral Change." *Psychological Review* 84, no. 2 (1977): 191–215.

Bortmas, Dominique. "Destroying Imposter Phenomenon in Code4Lib and Ourselves." Presentation at the Code4Lib Conference, Los Angeles, CA, March 7, 2017. https://drive.google.com/file/d/0B1ZWw7jPvbGfcE1KTGZmT0Qwd3M/view.

Carnevale, Anthony P., Jeff Strohl, and Michelle Melton. *What's It Worth?: The Economic Value of College Majors*. Washington, DC: Georgetown University Center on Education and the Workforce, 2014. https://cew.georgetown.edu/wp-content/uploads/2014/11/whatsit-worth-complete.pdf.

Chamberlain, Andrew. "Why Is Hiring Taking Longer? New Insights from Glassdoor Data," 2015. http://www.glassdoor.com/research/app/uploads/sites/2/2015/06/GD_Report_3.pdf.

Clance, Pauline Rose, and Suzanne Ament Imes. "The Imposter Phenomenon in High Achieving Women: Dynamics and Therapeutic Intervention." *Psychotherapy: Theory, Research & Practice* 15, no. 3 (1978): 241-247.

Corbett, Christianne, and Catherine Hill. *Solving the Equation: The Variables for Women's Success in Engineering and Computing.* Washington, DC: American Association of University Women, 2015.

Cuddy, Amy. "Your Body Language May Shape Who You Are." Filmed June 2012 in Edinburgh, Scotland. TED video, 20:56. https://www.ted.com/talks/amy_cuddy_your_body_language_shapes_who_you_are.

Department for Professional Employees, AFL-CIO. "Library Workers: Facts and Figures," n.d. http://dpeaflcio.org/programs-publications/issue-fact-sheets/library-workers-facts-figures/.

Deyrup, Marta. "Academic Library Leadership, Second Wave Feminism, and Twenty-First Century Humanism." In *Leadership in Academic Libraries Today: Connecting Theory to Practice,* edited by Bradford Lee Eden and Jody Condit Fagan. Lanham: Rowman & Littlefield, 2014.

Fisher, William. "The Question of Gender in Library Management." *Library Administration and Management* 11, no. 4 (1997): 231–36.

Golub, Erin Marie. "Gender Divide in Librarianship: Past, Present and Future." *Library Student Journal* 5 (2010).

Hackman, Rose. "'Women Are Just Better at This Stuff': Is Emotional Labor Feminism's next Frontier?" *The Guardian,* November 8, 2015. https://www.theguardian.com/world/2015/nov/08/women-gender-roles-se

Hanna, Kathleen. "RIOT GRRRL MANIFESTO." Accessed July 5, 2017. http://onewarart.org/riot_grrrl_manifesto.htm.

Harris, Roma M. "Gender and Technology Relations in Librarianship." *Journal of Education for Library and Information Science* 40, no. 4 (1999): 232–46.

Heilbronner, Nancy N. "Stepping onto the STEM Pathway: Factors Affecting Talented Students' Declaration of STEM Majors in College." *Journal for the Education of the Gifted* 34, no. 6 (2011): 876–99. https://doi.org/10.1177/0162353211425100.

Henn, Steve. "When Women Stopped Coding." Planet Money : NPR, October 21, 2014. https://www.npr.org/sections/money/2014/10/21/357629765/when-women-stopped-coding.

Hildenbrand, Suzanne. "The Information Age versus Gender Equity? Technology and Values in Education for Library and Information Science." *Library Trends* 47, no. 4 (1999): 669–85.

Hildenbrand, Suzanne. "The Information Age vs. Gender Equity." *Library Journal* 124, no. 7 (1999): 44–47.

Hooks, Bell. *Teaching Critical Thinking : Practical Wisdom.* New York: Routledge, 2010.

Hutchison, Christine. "Why Women Are Tired: The Price of Unpaid Emotional Labor." HuffPost (blog), April 6, 2016. https://www.huffingtonpost.com/psyched-in-san-francisco/why-women-are-tired-the-p_b_9619732.h

James, Deborah, and Sandra Clarke. "Women, Men, and Interruptions: A Critical Review." In *Gender and Conversational Interaction,* edited by Deborah Tannen, 231–80. New York: Oxford University Press, 1993.

Kay, Katty, and Claire Shipman. "The Confidence Gap." *The Atlantic,* May 2014. https://www.theatlantic.com/magazine/archive/2014/05/the-confidence-gap/359815/.

Lamont, Melissa. "Gender, Technology, and Libraries." *Information Technology and Libraries* 28, no. 3 (September 1, 2009): 137–142.

Lynch, Clifford. "From Automation to Transformation: Forty Years of Libraries and Information Technology in Higher Education." *Educause Review* 35, no. 1 (2000): 60–71.

Madera, Juan M., Michelle R. Hebl, and Randi C. Martin. "Gender and Letters of Recommendation for Academia: Agentic and Communal Differences." *Journal of Applied Psychology* 94, no. 6 (2009): 1591–99. https://doi.org/10.1037/a0016539.

Margolis, Jane, and Allan Fisher. *Unlocking the Clubhouse: Women in Computing.* Cambridge, MA: MIT Press, 2002.

Miller, Kevin. "The Simple Truth about the Gender Pay Gap." AAUW. Accessed January 19, 2018. https://www.aauw.org/research/the-simple-truth-about-the-gender-pay-gap/.

Mohr, Tara Sophia. "Why Women Don't Apply for Jobs Unless They're 100% Qualified." Harvard Business Review, 2014.

https://static1.squarespace.com/static/52f84192e4b0bae-912c881e6/t/564b37e6e4b03f66f2c62080/1447770086778/Why+Women+Dont+Apply+for+Jobs_HBR.pdf.

————. "Why Women Don't Apply for Jobs Unless They're 100% Qualified." *Harvard Business Review*, 2014. https://hbr.org/2014/08/why-women-dont-apply-for-jobs-unless-theyre-100-qualified.

Moore, Tracy. "Is It Even Worthwhile to Teach Men to Value Emotional Labor?" Jezebel (blog), November 15, 2015. https://jezebel.com/is-it-even-worthwhile-to-teach-men-to-value-emotional-l-1742222786.

Olin, Jessica, and Michelle Millet. "Gendered Expectations for Leadership in Libraries." *In the Library with the Lead Pipe*, November 4, 2015. http://www.inthelibrarywiththeleadpipe.org/2015/libleadgender/.

Phillips, Katherine W. "Gender and Racial Bias Is Systemic in the Sciences." *NYTimes.com*, June 11, 2015. https://www.nytimes.com/roomfordebate/2015/06/11/nobel-winning-sexism-in-the-lab/gender-and-rac

Ricigliano, Lori, and Renée Houston. "Men's Work, Women's Work: The Social Shaping of Technology in Academic Libraries." Paper presented at the Association of College and Research Libraries Eleventh National Conference, Charlotte, North Carolina, April 10-13, 2003, http://www.ala.org/acrl/sites/ala.org.acrl/files/content/conferences/pdf/ricigliano.PDF

Rohrmann, Sonja, Myriam N. Bechtoldt, and Mona Leonhardt. "Validation of the Impostor Phenomenon among Managers." *Frontiers in Psychology 7,* no. Jun(2016). https://doi.org/10.3389/fpsyg.2016.00821.

Sandberg, Sheryl, and Adam Grant. "Speaking While Female: Sheryl Sandberg and Adam Grant on Why Women Stay Quiet at Work." *The New York Times,* January 12, 2012. https://www.nytimes.com/2015/01/11/opinion/sunday/speaking-while-female.html

Schmader, Toni, Jessica Whitehead, and Vicki H. Wysocki. "A Linguistic Comparison of Letters of Recommendation for Male and Female Chemistry and Biochemistry Job Applicants." *Sex Roles* 57, no. 7–8 (2007) 509-514.

Simard, Caroline., Andrea Davies Henderson, Shannon K Gilmartin, Londa Schiebinger, and Telle Whitney. "Climbing the Technical Ladder: Obstacles and Solutions for Mid-Level Women in Technology," 2013. http://www.gedcouncil.org/sites/default/files/Climbing_the_Technical_Ladder.pdf.

Speer, S. C., and D. Angelucci. "Extending the Reach of the Thin Client." *Computers in Libraries* 21, no. 3 (2001): 46–50.

The College Board. "AP Data," n.d. https://research.collegeboard.org/programs/ap/data.

Thom, Kai Cheng. "8 Lessons That Show How Emotional Labor Defines Women's Lives." *Everyday Feminism, June 15, 2016.* https://everyday-feminism.com/2016/06/emotional-labor-womens-lives/.

Trauth, Eileen M., Jeria L. Quesenberry, and a J Morgan. "Understanding the under Representation of Women in IT: Toward a Theory of Individual Differences." *In 2004 ACM SIGMIS Conference on Computer Personnel Research: Careers, Culture, and Ethics in a Networked Environment,* 6:114–19, 2004.

Young, Valerie. *The Secret Thoughts of Successful Women: Why Capable People Suffer from the Impostor Syndrome and How to Thrive in Spite of It.* New York: Crown Business, 2011.

"Table 325.35: Degrees in Computer and Information Sciences Conferred by Postsecondary Institutions, by Level of Degree and Sex of Student: 1970-71 through 2014-15 (Excel File; 47 Kb)." *Digest of Education Statistics, 2016.* https://nces.ed.gov/programs/digest/d16/tables/dt16_325.35.asp.

"Women in Information Technology Interest Group." Library and Information Technology Association, n.d.

"LITA AvramCamp Preconference at the 2017 ALA Annual Conference in Chicago." Library and Information Technology Association (blog), March 31, 2017. http://litablog.org/2017/03/lita-adacamp-preconference-at-the-2017-ala-annual-conference-in-chicago/.

"Proving Competence and Challenging Stereotypes Are the Greatest Barriers Faced by Women in IT." Robert Half UK, September 29, 2016. https://www.roberthalf.co.uk/press/proving-competence-and-challenging-stereotypes-are-greatest-barriers-faced-women-it.

"Computer and Information Technology Occupations." United States Department of Labor Women's Bureau, last modified July, 2015. https://www.dol.gov/wb/stats/Computer_information_technology_2014.htm.

"Women in Drupal (Formerly DrupalChix)." Drupal Groups, n.d. https://groups.drupal.org/women-drupal.

"2017 Drupal Association at-Large Election Winner Announced." Drupal Association (blog), March

27, 2017. https://www.drupal.org/association/
blog/2017-drupal-association-at-large-election-winner-announced.

"Ars Technica." WIRED Media Group, n.d. https://arstechnica.com.

"Slashdot." SlashdotMedia, n.d. slashdot.org.

"Landing Party : Free Download and Streaming : Internet Archive."
Accessed January 19, 2018. https://archive.org/details/
msdos_Landing_Party_1989.

"Chimera." *Wikipedia*, January 18, 2018. https://en.wikipedia.
org/wiki/Chimera.

"Girls Who Code." Girls Who Code, n.d. https://girlswhocode.com/.

"LibTechWomen," n.d. http://libtechwomen.org.

"ARL Annual Salary Survey 2014–2015." Association of Research
Libraries. Washington, DC, 2015. http://publications.arl.org/
ARL-Annual-Salary-Survey-2014-2015.

"Trends in the State of Computer Science in U.S. K-12 Schools," 2016.
http://goo.gl/j291E0.

"Women in Information Technology." Library Information Technology
Association (LITA), n.d. http://www.ala.org/lita/about/igs/
women-in-information-technology/lit-igwiit.